If Christ were standing here with us, how should we feel, not about him, but about ourselves?
—*Saint Augustine*

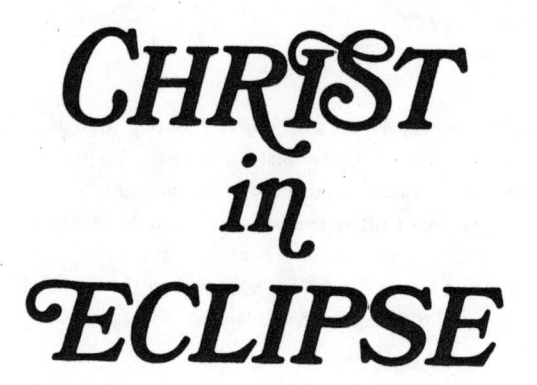

CHRIST in ECLIPSE

A Clinical Study of the Good Christian

2 32
she

F. J. Sheed

SHEED ANDREWS AND McMEEL, INC.
Subsidiary of Universal Press Syndicate
KANSAS CITY

1st Printing, May 1978
2nd Printing, August 1978

Library of Congress Cataloging in Publication Data
Sheed, Francis Joseph, 1897-
    Christ in eclipse.

    1. Jesus Christ — Person and offices.   2. Chris-
tian life — Catholic authors. I. Title.

BT202.S46   232   78-5077
ISBN 0-8362-3302-6

*DEDICATED
TO
ALL WHO EARN
FULL MARKS
ON
CHAPTER ONE*

Contents

Foreword

For the last ten years a feeling has been growing in me that there is something strange in the attitude of Christians to Christ Our Lord. At first I took it lightly because no one else seemed to have noticed it. I read the documents of Vatican II closely but could find no hint of awareness of it. But the feeling grew steadily stronger of what I have found myself calling the absence of Christ.

In an age of Eucharistic Congresses, TV shows watched by millions, vast open-air Masses, the notion sounded like insanity. But it persisted, and slowly I came to see more precisely what was troubling me. At a lecture in Madras I stated it, asking the audience to see how far it matched their own experience. In essence it was this—that genuinely committed Christians, Catholics and Protestants, revere Christ, try to live up to his teachings, received him sacramentally, hope they would die rather than deny him—but do not in fact find him very interesting, or his message meeting any needs they are aware of in themselves.

I chose my words with care, because the idea was new to the audience and could easily be misunderstood. I was not questioning their faith or their devotion. But it is possible to live an active, even dedicated, Christian life without very much direct awareness of Christ himself, without indeed giving very much thought to him. Church or sacraments or liturgical music or service to one's fellow men or women can fill the mind's foreground, while Christ himself is a revered presence in a depth of the mind that one seldom visits. We might be living in his service, yet not know him any better than we knew him as children. He is not absent, but he is surely in eclipse.

What the audience made of all this, I could not be sure. I had asked them to test what I was saying by their own experience. I fancy they needed to go home and think about it. The *Catholic Leader* of Madras gave a clear account of the condition I had been describing. They called it Sheed's Disease—as it might be Bright's or Parkinson's—not meaning I was suffering from it but that I had isolated and analyzed it.

At least so I supposed. Slowly I came to see that I was letting myself off too lightly. I don't know if Bright was ever a victim of his disease, or Parkinson, but Sheed shows all too many symptoms of his. Which of us does not?

That is what this book is about—*How real is Christ to us, how well do we know him, what strong desire have we to know him better?*

Upon that, each chapter is an examination—not exactly of our conscience, but of our consciousness, our awareness, of Christ. Thus basically it *is* an examination of conscience, deeper than our usual scamper over the day's deeds. Each chapter raises questions—sometimes *as* questions, sometimes as truths which ought to be known—which will help us to diagnose our own case: this is one disease whose hold on us only ourselves can know: and only if we want to. You will not often find a book in which there are so many probing questions—not the kind a teacher asks his pupils, but the kind a doctor asks his patients.

I have dedicated it to *All Who Earn Full Marks On Chapter One*. I envy them.

All the same, I am not writing my confessions. If occasionally something gives you the feeling that what I am saying bites too close for my own comfort, I hope you will be wrong.

PART ONE
Meeting Christ

How Real Is Christ to Us?

1.

On Good Friday we commemorate Christ's death, on Easter Sunday his Resurrection. In the lives of most Christians these are the high points. Do we only feel them as history, or do we see them as affecting us here and now? He conquered sin and death, Scripture tells us. But we know that we shall die, sin shows no sign of losing its grip.

Paul tells the Corinthians that if Christ had not risen, they and he would be the most miserable of men: but many learned Christian teachers are denying the Resurrection, their happiness not noticeably affected: does Paul's word "miserable" say anything at all to you and me?

With the explosion of the sixties, these questions became urgent for Catholics and Protestants alike. It left no Church as it had been before. But the effect on the Catholic Church was the most spectacular, because it had seemed for so long so monolithic, so invulnerable. I shall pause on it for a short while—the problems of all the Churches can be seen in it as in a larger mirror. Besides, I can speak more freely of the defects of my fellow Catholics.

Up to the death of Pius XII, in 1958, things went serenely enough for the mass of Catholics. There were

3

theologians working on the frontiers of doctrine and others on the very roots, but their writings caused no alarm for they did not reach most of us. There were Catholics dropping out, but they usually went quietly, just let go: and there were no statistics published or even compiled of their fading out.

When John XXIII became pope, we reminded ourselves that at his age he could be only a stopgap, giving the Church a breathing space in which to consider any changes that might seem necessary. Breathing space? We have hardly breathed since. The explosion came at once. The questioning by theologians of every doctrine at last reached the surface where the laity live. It came first in the form of changes in practices long established—the Mass rewritten, Benediction abolished, Latin thrown out, Friday abstinence gone and Lenten fasting, confession soft-pedaled—more changes in the two decades since Pius XII's death than in the four hundred years since the Council of Trent—with eager reformers accusing Rome of dragging its feet.

The result was a great cleavage in the Catholic ranks. There are conservatives who hate the changes, feeling that what they had been accustomed to *was* the Faith, that they had lost something precious. There are radicals who welcome changes, can't wait for more of them. The extremists on both sides have two things in common.

One is a sketchy knowledge of history, with little idea of the sheer multiplicity of changes through the centuries. As an example, take the practice of placing the consecrated host in the hand instead of on the tongue. This was disliked by the conservatives as an innovation, welcomed by radicals as an innovation—a first step perhaps for some of them on the way to having each one do his own consecrating. About the newness they were both wrong. It had been practiced in the early Church, only dying out in the seventh century—to the anguish perhaps of seventh-century conservatives. More to the point in our present inquiry is the second quality that conservatives and radicals seem to share—a way of discussing both the present situation and proposed changes without reference to Christ, simply forming their own view of what needs doing, and either not adverting to Christ or assuming his agreement.

Consider the numbers—reduced now, but a few years back approaching flood level—of priests pouring out of her. In my travels and at home I have read scores of statements by them, and how rarely is Christ mentioned, save perfunctorily and in passing. Yet he must have figured vastly in their decision to become priests and in the serving of their flock. Quite apart from priesthood, surely the one reason anyone has for belonging to the Catholic or any other Church is the conviction that Christ wants him there. It is strange to leave without relating one's action to him—with not so much as Peter's "to whom else shall we go?"

In the criticisms uttered by many who do not get around to leaving the Church there is the same failure to see him as the whole point. So much in its daily running they find depressing—the sermons, they say, take no one deeper into the reality of God or man; this priest or that cares for nothing but money, the sick neglected, the old rejected; the hierarchy know nothing of the emotional or intellectual problems which are eating away at the vitality of their people's faith, the Curia is simply a bureaucracy, using every trick to hold on to its power; as for the pope . . . . It all adds up to "the Institutional Church," with so many wondering if their spiritual integrity will permit them to remain in it.

I am meeting this wherever I go. I have fallen into the way of reminding the objector that Institutional Israel, the Chosen People, as the Prophets show it, was even worse than the harshest critics think the Catholic Church: yet it never occurred to the holiest of the Jews to leave it. They knew that however evilly the administration behaved, Israel was still the people of God. So with the Church: an administration is necessary if the Church is to function, but Christ is the whole point of the functioning. We are not baptized into the hierarchy, do not receive the cardinals sacramentally, will not spend eternity in the beatific vision of the pope. St. John Fisher could say in a public sermon, "If the Pope will not reform the Curia, God will": a couple of years later he laid his head on Henry VIII's block for papal supremacy, followed to the same block by Thomas More, who had spent his youth under the Borgia pope, Alexander VI, lived his early manhood under the Medici pope, Leo X, and died for papal supremacy under Clement VII, as time-serving a pope as Rome had had.

Christ *is* the point. I myself admire the present pope, Paul VI; but even if I criticized him as harshly as some do, even if his successor proved to be as bad as some of those who have gone before, even if I sometimes find the Church as I have to live in it a pain in the neck, I should still say that nothing a pope could do or say would make me wish to leave the Church, though I might well wish that *he* would. Israel, through its best periods as through its worst, preserved the truth of God's Oneness in a world swarming with gods and the sense of God's majesty in a world sick with its own pride. So with the Church. Under the worst administration—say as bad as John XII's a thousand years ago—we could still learn Christ's truth, receive his life in the sacraments, be in union with him to the limit of our willingness. In awareness of Christ, I can know the Church as his Mystical Body. And we must not make our judgments by the neck's sensitivity to pain!

2.

Most of what we have just been looking at is of interest mainly to Catholics. We come now to two matters of more general interest—the Mass, which concerns all but extreme Protestants; the next life, which concerns all of us without exception.

The first matter on which the laity took alarm was the announcement of changes in the offering of Mass: even the least observant could not be unaware of them. I was present at scores of discussions, both formal and as it chanced, about Latin or vernacular, the untouchability of the Tridentine Mass, whether the priest should wear vestments or overalls, whether Mass is better celebrated in church or at the kitchen table. In none of these discussions did serenity rule: I had never seen so many Catholics so worked up about a religious question. But this was the first period in which I clearly felt that absence of Christ of which I have talked. I never heard his name mentioned in any of these discussions, either by those who loathed the changes or by those who reveled in them.

Realize how strange that is. Mass is not simply a memorial of one who died long ago, culminating in a reception of the Eucharist. We are not just being present while the priest is doing his consecrating at the altar. Priest and we are joining with Christ in something he is *now* doing in heaven. Calvary was complete: but we learn (Rom. 8:24, Heb. 7:24) that Christ, at the Father's right hand, continues to intercede for us. There he offers himself, once slain on Calvary, now forever living, to his Father that the salvation he had won for our race should be taken and made their own by every one of the race's members. At the altar, the priest, *and we with him,* offer the same Christ, sacramentally present, to the same Father, for the same purpose. At Mass, Christ's continuing action in heaven breaks through to our altars.

Changes in the Mass were discussed without considering what Christ might think of them—not only not mentioning him, apparently not even adverting to him. Is absence too strong a word for that? It certainly is no very full presence.

At the Last Supper Christ said to the Apostles, "I go to prepare a place for you, that *where I am, you may be.*" It is worth asking ourselves if that thought stands high in our minds, either when a friend dies, or when something forces our mind to linger briefly on the certainty that we too will one day die. Upon this, as upon all the other self-questions raised in this chapter, it is of some urgency that we should not fool ourselves.

The chances are that in neither instance does the meeting with Christ loom large. We may think of the dead friend as reunited with people he loved. We may go on to think of ourselves meeting some of history's more interesting people, Napoleon, perhaps, or Shakespeare, not lingering too long on the question of whether they are likely to be where we ourselves hope to go.

St. Paul would have liked to die sooner in order to be with Christ sooner (Phil. 1:24). We need not blame ourselves for not feeling Christ's reality as intensely as Paul, who had been in spectacular contact with him on the road to Damascus. But it is well worth our while, even if we are devoted Christians, to ask ourselves in all seriousness—do we look forward with any pleasure at all to meeting him in heaven? If the thought brings no stimulation with it, then it looks as if we have been taking him for granted too long without giving very much of our mind to him. And we hardly need to be told what effect that sort of treatment would have on our friendship with anyone at all.

We have been asking ourselves how real Christ is to us in relation to the Church, the Mass, heaven. These three concern us closely—the Church is the context of our life with him; Mass is the most important thing we ever do; we all have to die. The merest self-interest would seem to dictate a Christ-interest.

Now for a rather different question—what interest have we in the things that interested him, but do not directly or unmistakably affect us? There is no surer test of his reality in our minds. And there is no doubt at all of what mattered

most to Christ—his Father. The first word we hear from
him is, "Didn't you know that I must be in my Father's
house?" The last word before he died on the Cross was,
"Father, into thy hands I commend my spirit." The first
message he sent to the Apostles after his Resurrection
was, "I ascend to my Father and your Father, to my God
and your God." A good hundred times we find him talking
of or to his Father. He makes him the object of his own
life—"I do the will of him that sent me"; he makes him the
object of ours—"No one comes to the Father but by me."
At death our welcome will be, "Enter into the joy of my
Father." When he is asked, "Teach us to pray," he tells us
to begin, "Our Father who art in heaven." Nothing special about that, we may think—unless we happen to know
that while the Jews saw God as a loving father, it was not
their way to address him as Father. In all the Old Testament we meet no prayer beginning with those two words.
Nor indeed did it come easy to the New Christians. There
is no account in the New Testament of any of them saying
it.

If what interests Christ does not interest us, the question arises how much he himself interests us. How much
thought do we give to his Father—do we even get as far as
wondering what meaning there is in a pure spirit having a
son? Is Father simply the first name in a refrain, "Father,
Son, and Holy Spirit"? If so, what of the third name, Holy
Spirit? Forty times the New Testament speaks of God as
threefold, and Spirit is always there. One of those utterances we all know—"Baptizing them in the name of the
Father and of the Son and of the Holy Spirit." Do we
wonder what the third one is doing in such august com-

pany? Given that Father and Son are each holy and each spirit, do we even get as far as wondering why the third should be called Holy Spirit? We can be singularly incurious.

When the Apostles were desolated to be told that Christ was leaving them to go to his Father, the explanation he gave was, "If I do not go, the Spirit will not come" (John 16:7). Who and what was this Spirit, whose coming was to be sufficient compensation for the loss of Christ's presence among them?

3.

Trinity, Church, Mass, heaven—these are high matters. We may not give much thought to Christ in regard to any of them because they are not part of our daily world, not that we lack interest in Christ, but in them. We may live our own lives close to the ground. Even in that circumscribed world he could be real to us—men and women have died for him who knew him only in the dailiness of their lives: and short of martyrdom one has met people who say things which prove they are seeing him rich and deep.

For them as for Christians of wider horizons, there are certain acid tests. When questions arise as to what we should believe about hell, for instance, still more as to how we should behave about sex, say, or the use of money, it is possible for Christians at every level to think out their own solutions without its ever occurring to them to ask what Christ's teaching on the question might have been: they possess a general notion of Christianity—a combination of what they remember having heard in

church with what they see as their own best self: by this
they feel they know what Christ would have said without
any need to ask what he did say. It often works well
enough, but with a strong dash of wishful thinking. We
might ask ourselves how long it is since we last made a
decision because of Christ which cost us heavily. When
did we last give a gift of money which meant denying
ourselves something we badly wanted?

A really frightening test of how much value we attach to
him lies in how we feel about friends who never seem to
give him a thought. Do we feel it as unbearable that they
should not have the gifts of light and nourishment that he
has given us? If not, we should ask ourselves how much
those same gifts do actually mean to ourselves?

If we are not longing to make him known, then he may
well be no more than a picture on the wall of our minds to
which we give a respectful bow when we happen to notice
it. If there were a famine and people lacked bread, we
should work hard to relieve it. But if they lack the Bread of
Life and it causes not the faintest stirring in us even of care
much less of desire to aid their destitution—we have to
ask ourselves what that tells us about ourselves. How
much does their starvation matter to us? Do we even
think of it as starvation? Even if we felt like helping, how
competent should we be to instruct anyone about Christ
himself or any of his teaching?

When we are hesitating about the rightness or wrong-
ness of something we feel a strong urge to do, do we ask
ourselves whether we could tell it to Christ? Remember
Augustine's grim question—"If Christ were standing here

with us, what should we feel, not about him, but about ourselves?"

We know what one man felt about himself in the presence of Christ—Peter had cried out, "Depart from me, Lord, for I am a sinful man" (Luke 5:8): as so often, Peter said the wrong thing—as if we were to say to a doctor, "Please go away, I'm sick." But which of us would not have had the same first reaction as Peter? And Augustine knew that the answer to his second question depends on the answer to the first: What do we, in naked fact, feel about Christ?

Ogden Nash wrote a poem (shall we call it?) about how he might lose the girl he loved when she was away in France—

> *Men of the world with etchings and monocles*
> *Plead with her to become part of their chronicles.*

The last four words are what Christ should be for all of us. Apart from the world we share with the human race, each one has his own individual world, the world actually present to him, the world in which he does his own daily living, its elements never far from his consciousness—his wife and family, parents and friends, his job and his wages, his employer and his workmates, his debts, the roof that needs mending, his politics and his amusements, the weather; in this world his personal chronicle unfolds. Christ should be part of it.

A simple test is how often we think of him in the course of the day. We may or may not say morning and night prayers, may or may not get to Mass on weekdays. If we do, are they just a routine carried over from childhood with most of the living element drained out or do we look forward to them as real conversation with Christ and his Father? If only we could put as much of ourself into adoration and gratitude as we put into our praying for what we want! Apart from prayers at set times, there are what used to be called ejaculatory prayers—"My Jesus mercy," for instance. They are short, not all of them suit all tastes, but they are reminders of him which help to keep the contact alive.

The ordinary business of living means that we cannot do much of all this. But if we never do any of it, we are missing what Bach calls Jesus—the "joy of man's desiring." That very phrase could stir us alive. We may love the music, but what joy have we in Jesus? How much desiring? At a lower level, take

> *Jesus lover of my soul*
> *Let me to thy bosom flee.*

We might not feel much like singing that now—bosom has become a comic word, and flee is sure of a laugh. But could we write our own feeling about Jesus better? Our own feeling.

All the questions we have been considering depend upon what we do in fact feel about him. How often do we think of him? How much do we want his company here and hereafter? How much does it mean to us that in Mass we are offering Calvary along with him? How far do his gifts of life and light and food and union outweigh the defects of the Institutional Church? Your personal answers and mine to all these depend on how much he means to us. And that *must* be related to how well we know him.

"Come unto me all you who labor and are heavy burdened, and I will give you rest" (Matt. 11:28). Heaven knows how laborious our life is, yours and mine, and how heavy the burdens we must carry. But do we think of Christ as helping us to bear them? He wants our company. Do we want his?

If our answer to that question leaves us depressed, what should we do about it? Certainly we should not try to whip ourselves into an emotional frenzy—thinking of his compassion for men, say, or his agony in Gethsemane, or his facing and outfacing death on Calvary, and accusing ourselves of heartlessness for not being grief-stricken.

That is more likely to lead to religious hysteria ending in despair. The better way is to forget ourselves, and simply concentrate on getting to know his words and his works and his very self, better and better. Out of that kind of growth in knowledge, love grows naturally. Most of us must have had the experience of working with someone over a long space, liking him but not giving a great deal of thought to him personally; and quite suddenly some accidental happening shows us how much he really means to us, how great our devotion to him. That is the experience we can have if we live with Christ in the Gospels.

Postscript

You have probably heard the story of the Catholic who,

asked if he went to Mass on Sundays, said, "I'm a
Catholic, not a fanatic." I can imagine readers feeling like
that about the chapter just ended. And that too would be
an answer. But if that is the way you feel, have a good long
look at that feeling before just sinking back into it. You
might even look through the questions and put a mark
against any to which you think even a nonfanatical Christian ought to be able to say Yes.

CHAPTER TWO

On Thinking We Are Reading The Gospels

Reading the Gospels is not the only way of growing into the knowledge of Christ: there is the teaching of the Church—whether for good or ill he is gentler in her teaching than in the Gospels. There is the living of his revelation, prayer to Father and Holy Spirit, Mass, sacraments—and all the endless ways of loving God and loving our neighbor.

But without the Gospels it is hard to grow into intimacy with Christ, which like all intimacy must be our own. Two of us might know a third equally well, yet if each wrote a personality sketch, each might surprise the other. No one responds to every element in another, least of all in a person at once so like us as Christ and so toweringly beyond us. We respond to different elements in him, or respond differently to the same elements, according to our own interests, knowledge, ignorance, attractions, repulsions, sensitivities, obliquities.

But that is all part of the growing process. The intimacy resultant rises beyond it and has an existence in its own right as a contact between the living reality that is oneself and the living reality that is Christ. It cannot be taught. It can only be our own personal growth into possession: for each of us this possession is the truth about us and Christ, and so about us and God.

For the building of our intimacy, we read Matthew,
Mark, Luke, and John as men and women have seen his
face in them for nineteen hundred years. Once we are
really at home in them, then the teaching of the Church
and the speculating whereby theologians move toward
deeper understanding, will give a new dimension to our
closeness.

1.

Even concerned Christians can fall into a habit of reading Scripture in a state of pious coma. They feel it is
inspiring, ennobling, all of which it is. They hear the
words but they may have little mental concentration on
what is actually being said.

Take an example or two.

They hear Peter urging Jesus not to go through with the
suffering and dying which he had told the Apostles
awaited him in Jerusalem (Matt. 16:22). They hear the
fierceness of Jesus' reply to Peter: "Get thee behind me,
Satan! You are a stumbling block to me; for you are not on
the side of God but of men." This just after he told Peter
that he was the rock on which Jesus would build his
Church, and that Jesus would give him the keys of the
Kingdom of Heaven! In no depth of coma could the reader
fail to see the contrast: only if he sees *both* the rebuke,
"Get behind me, Satan!" and the promise, "On this rock,"
will he begin to understand the history of the papacy.

But when he hears Jesus in the Garden of his Agony
pleading with his Father, "If it be possible, let this cup
pass from me," does it occur to him that Jesus seems to be

making the same plea to his Father which he had called satanic when Peter urged it on him? As we shall see, there is a deeper answer: but if the verbal similarity had not struck him, if he has not seen that he was in the presence of something demanding explanation, then, pious or not, he is in coma's grip. He has not really been *reading* at all.

One thinks of a dozen examples of this sort of failure to respond to what is actually there. When, defending the papacy, we point out that Christ has made Peter the rock on which he would build his Church, someone is sure to object, "Paul said the rock was Christ." It is rare to find a Catholic who knows that Paul said it (1 Cor. 10:4). I have even put it to classes on the afternoon of Septuagesima Sunday, and none recognized it, though it had been read aloud at Mass that morning. Had they not been too deep in coma, Paul's phrase would have startled them wide awake: for he was talking of a very different rock, the rock from which Moses drew water in the desert twelve hundred years before: and he said that that rock was Christ.

Back to the Gospels. From the Cross, Jesus told his Mother and John that from now on they were to be mother and son. If the reader thinks the episode was no more than a sensible provision for his Mother's welfare, then his intelligence is not in action (how different the small boy who blamed Joseph for *not booking ahead* in Bethlehem). Christ had known that he was close to death; why did he leave this till Calvary? It could not have been a sudden remembering of a small matter he had managed to overlook. Why did he decide that that was the place to say it? At least there is a question—whether or not my own feeling is correct that Christ's every word and action on the Cross belonged in the sacrifice of our redemption: and that Mary has a part in its continuance.

Reading is not just taking words off a page into the head. The written word can go in one eye and out the other as automatically as the spoken word can use the ears, leaving the mind undisturbed and unaware.

2.

There is a nonpious coma too; let's call it protective, a way of not hearing what would disturb our comfort. There are two areas in which failure to take sin as seriously as Christ takes it raises a real question of whether we can read—our unreadiness to forgive and our attitude to wealth. In each we know just what he said, and we act as if he had not spoken or at least as if he could not possibly have meant *us*.

In the Lord's Prayer, which he gave in answer to his disciples' request for a lesson in praying, we ask God to forgive us our failures as we forgive those who fail us. We can say it daily without seeming to realize that we are asking God *not* to forgive us *if* we don't forgive. In other words we are not merely consenting to the dependence of our salvation on our willingness to forgive, but reminding God of it—yet not really reminding ourselves! And almost as if he saw that we should find it difficult to realize what we had said, the first comment he made as he finished the prayer was, "If you don't forgive, you won't be forgiven" (Matt. 6:15).

Not only do we not make a serious effort in this matter

but we seem to be wholly unaware that we ought to. There is un-wisdom in not taking seriously anything to which Christ says "Unless. . . ." Unless one is born again. . . unless you shall eat the flesh of the Son of Man . . . unless you shall forgive . . . . How sane are we?

The question of our sanity is raised even more depressingly by our attitude to wealth. There is nothing Christ warns us about more frequently or more emphatically than wealth's danger. He does this not primarily on account of wealth's exploitation of the poor but of its danger to the soul.

"If you serve money, you cannot serve God." He says that twice (Matt. 6:24 and Luke 16:13). He reminds us that the time we spend and the effort we expend in making and keeping money prevent all concentration on the soul's higher powers.

"The cares of the world and delight in riches choke the word so that it proves unfruitful" (Mark 4:19)—that is, wealth can sterilize.

"They are stifled by the cares, riches and pleasures of life and never reach maturity" (Luke 8:14)—that is, wealth can stunt.

And what is the result of the stunting and sterilizing? "It is easier for a camel to get through the eye of a needle than for a rich man to enter the Kingdom of Heaven." All three synoptists have this—Matthew in chapter 19, Mark in chapter 10, Luke in chapter 18.

Believers who happen to be rich have two quite different ways of sugaring this to their taste or sandpapering it to a more comfortable smoothness. One way of smoothing is to say that "needle's eye" was the name of a smaller gate in the wall of Jerusalem: so that a camel would find it difficult to get through—difficult, but not of course impossible—with a little wriggling. Another is to say that Christ did not mean it to be taken literally; he exaggerates to make sure that his warning against wealth's dangers may be sure to sink in. He does indeed sometimes use the figure we call hyperbole, it was normal in Jewish speech and writing.

But what actually followed the camel text makes both evasions impossible, and all three synoptists have this too. The Apostles, assuming that Christ meant it in all its starkness, said, "Then it is impossible for a rich man to be saved." There was nothing in his answer to make what he had said more palatable—"To man it is impossible, but to God all things are possible"—even the salvation of the rich.

Yet which of us would not like to be rich?

Indeed we who are not rich have our own way of at once hearing and not hearing something Christ directed straight at us—*If you don't help the poor in their need, you'll go to hell* (Matt. 25:32-46). All that actually reaches us of this is that when all our own needs are met Christ would like us to give some of the surplus to the needy. Certainly the threat of hell does not reach us. "Depart from me, you cursed, into the everlasting fire prepared for the devil and his angels"—we hear the words, but they could not conceivably be meant for the kindly people we know we are. But Christ's identification of himself with the neediest at the end of this section it is hard to believe that we have even heard (Matt. 25:42). "I was hungry and you did not give me to eat, thirsty and you did not give me to drink. I was a stranger, and you did not take me in, naked and you did not cover me, sick and in prison and you did not visit me. . . . As long as you didn't do these things to one of these least, neither did you do it to me."

For our own daily living these are the most terrifying words ever to issue from his lips. There are people destitute in our own country, hundreds of millions are living in subanimal conditions in the rest of the world—it is hard to believe that in our deciding what is called for from ourselves, we remember that we are deciding just how much we feel like giving *to and for Christ?*

One more example of nonpious coma, before we leave this depressing area of our devitalized listening. It is in Matthew 18 and Luke 15. A man with a hundred sheep loses one: he leaves the ninety-nine to look after themselves and goes to search for the lost one, and having found it rejoices more over that one than over all the rest. That in our world the proportion between the lost and the unlost has changed fearfully for the worse does not alter the moral. As it happens I have never heard a sermon on it. But in the general running of the Church where I have lived, I get the impression that the Good Shepherd might as well never have said it.

Even for us who are not shepherds, the passage has challenge. In the nature of things we meet more lost sheep, people who have lost contact with Christ, than the clergy meet. There is not much doubt what our Saviour would like us to do about them.

3.

I have spoken of coma pious and coma nonpious. But there is a third coma which can keep us from meeting the Christ of the Gospels—it is a passive acceptance of the Christ other people think they have seen. We must let no one impose on us his image of Christ. There seems to be no end to the pseudoimages. They seem to arise, most of them, from the sheer force of his personality.

We see it in action when he was on earth. It was not the "whip of small cords" that drove from the court of the Temple all those men hot on money who were making his Father's house a den of thieves. It was something in himself, the same something, perhaps, which enabled him to pass "through the midst" of the men of his own city when they would have "thrown him headlong over the cliff" on which Nazareth stood (Luke 3:30); the same something which caused the armed guard in Gethsemane to fall to the ground when he came toward them and said, "I am he" (John 18:5).

We cannot read John's account of his trial without feeling that Pilate felt it too. He could not often have heard a prisoner in Jesus' condition say, "You would have no power over me unless it were given you from on high, therefore he that delivered me to you has the greater sin."

The full power of his personality still makes itself felt, and not only by those to whom he is the name above every name (Phil. 2:9). We are continually finding people who do not accept him but cannot leave him alone.

There are scholars, for example, who devote an immense labor of study to leave us wondering why they

thought him worth studying, who write books which de-
hydrate him down to something not worth having—
certainly not worth all the energy they have poured out on
him. We find writers who strip him down to the bare
kerygma, the announcement of the good news of salvation; other writers who dekerygmatize him out of even
that. There is a whole splendor of thinking and writing
about him by unbelieving scholars. But why do they
bother? The Christ of so many of them has no life in him,
would have been kicked to death by the money-changers,
dismissed in ten seconds by Pilate, would not have men
dying for him today as they have through nineteen centuries. Who would have died for the Christ one has met
him reduced to?

Then there are the practical men, not usually scholars,
who feel that their cause, whatever it is, will be richer for
having his name inscribed on its banners and himself
shown marching under them. Many with the sketchiest
knowledge and no habit of Bible reading to enrich the
knowledge, build their own ideals and indignations into
an image that they call Christ, so that he is turned into a
propaganda weapon, and his name into a slogan.

Thus, for his own first followers, he was Christ, the
anointed one, the Messiah who should restore the kingdom to Israel. In our own day we have Christ the proletarian revolutionary bent upon the overthrowing of the rich.

Pause upon that: it is urged so vehemently that not to
be a proletarian revolutionary is a betrayal of Christ, that a
reader might read the Gospels from end to end never
doubting that that is the Christ he is meeting, never
noticing that of political, social, economic revolution he

finds not a word. I have even heard people quote:

> He has put down the mighty from their thrones
> And exalted those of low degree;
> He has filled the hungry with good things
> And the rich he has sent empty away—

—but that was not said by Christ but by his Mother.

Any one of us could so easily have mapped out for him a program of really valid and viable revolution that we might feel it a solid question mark against him that he not only did none of it but preached none of it. There was the indefensible occupation by pagan Romans of the Jewish homeland: he joined no Jewish Liberation Front, though there was one—he may even have drawn one of the Twelve, Simon Zelotes, out of it; of slavery, then still existent in the Jewish community, we hear no word from him.

He is indeed on the side of the poor, and he condemns the rich. But, disappointingly you may think, he does not set them against each other—even when he gets the two into a single parable (Luke 16:20). Do read the parable. The rich man "feasted sumptuously every day." Lazarus clutched at such food as "fell from the other's table: moreover the dogs came and licked his sores." The poor man "died and was carried by angels to Abraham's bosom." Pause on that. We are not to think of Lazarus as sitting in Abraham's lap, no comfortable posture for two grown men: the phrase "Abraham's bosom" means that he reclined at the banquet table in the place of honor, next to

Abraham himself, the father of the Jewish people. The rich man "died and was buried: and in Hades, in a torment of thirst," he begged that Lazarus be sent "to dip the end of his finger in water, and cool my tongue." Read on to the end of the parable.

Observe that Christ does indeed condemn the rich—only God's omnipotence can save them. But not so much for their exploitation of the poor. Lazarus was not the rich man's employee. The radical fault he finds in them is their total concentration on self, a self concerned only with this world. "Woe to you rich, you have your consolations" (Luke 6:24).

Once you have grasped him, you may very well feel that political social revolution *is* the moral to be drawn from the whole of his teaching, but at least be aware that you do not find him drawing that moral for you. You may feel that he would want you to agitate for civil rights, you may marvel that the Evangelists left it out. But leave it out they did.

Nor do we find him giving any blueprint of a social economic system, not so much as a hint of how it would be structured. (Save that those in charge must serve the rest, he leaves the structuring to us.) But "he knew the heart of man": he did not need the future to tell him that, unless the heart is healed, nationalist revolutions, throwing out the foreigner, will mean that people will be exploited by men of their own nation just as ruthlessly; and proletarian revolutions will mean a change of exploiters within the same nation.

Unless the heart is healed.

4.

Both read the Bible day and night
But thou read'st black where I read white.

The problem Blake states here has always faced Christians. Each must solve it as best he can: a Catholic knows what provision he thinks Christ made toward its solving.

But today the plain man finds what looks like a new barrier interposed between himself and what the Gospels have to tell about Christ, the theorizing of the Scripture scholars. He does not read them, for he has not the learning or the linguistic training to cope with them. He meets them, boiled down for shock value, in his daily and weekly papers; he may meet them in the pulpit on Sundays.

The latest findings of the most learned Scripture scholarship are being thrust by journalists, who themselves do not know the Scriptures very well, on people who do not know them at all. The result is that our plain man feels he cannot safely believe anything he has ever thought he knew about Christ. He is left feeling like Mary Magdalene—"They have taken away my Lord and I know not where they have laid him."

For the special purpose of this book he need not worry. Most of the matters we are concerned with still stand— the main lines of Christ's public life, what we may call his personality, his values and priorities, the guidance he gives about life as we should live it. And they are enough for our first movement into intimacy and our growth in it. All the rest of our discipleship depends upon it: without it, however learned one or other of us may be, we are merely skating on the surface, the depth in ourselves in no contact with the depth in him.

We must find our way about the Gospels, make ourselves at home in them—knowing, for instance, what each of the Evangelists has set out to do—Mark to give us the "gospel of Jesus Christ, the Son of God," as he had heard Peter preach it; Matthew to show the universal Church growing out of Israel; Luke to show it growing into the whole world; John that we "may know that Jesus is the Christ, the Son of God, and that believing we may have life in his Name." Thus we find ourselves meeting intimately the same Christ, but as portrayed from different angles by very different artists.

Given that, we can enrich our intimacy with what both the Church and the scholars have to offer us. In nineteen centuries the Church's definitions have thrown great rays of light into the central mystery, light which for too many of us is only darkness made darker, rich formulas with all their richness locked up in them for those who do not know Christ himself.

Knowing what the Gospels show Christ doing and saying, we can read what the scholars write—their different interpretations, for instance, of passages whose meanings we had taken for granted, their rejection as interpolations of passages we love—and make up our own minds in all serenity. We can profit by their knowledge of history, language, literature, and such. We give them our ears, gratefully, but not our minds. For they also are conditioned as we are by interests, ignorance, needs, attractions, repulsions, sensitivities, obliquities.

If we have no more than a nodding acquaintance with the Gospel Christ, then the scholars can muddle us, theology can numb us.

The people were marveling at Christ's learning, considering that "he had never studied"—i.e., he had not gone to the best schools, not been taught by the most famous rabbis—in fact hadn't his union card! Jesus answered: "My teaching is not mine, but his who sent me. If any man is to do (God's) will, he shall know whether the teaching is from God or whether I am speaking on my own authority" (John 7:16-17).

Learning is not the whole thing. We still, like St. Paul's Christians, have not many "wise among us by earthly standards." And Christ's rule is forever valid, that those who live the life have in themselves the irreplaceable essential for intimacy. And even the best schools cannot test their students for that.

Postscript

1.

There are difficulties in Gospel reading because there are differences in Gospel writing. I note four of the more obvious.

a) There is the use of numbers. For us they belong to arithmetic, for them they belonged to rhetoric.

The ages of the patriarchs, for instance, mean that the writers saw their ancestors as greater men than themselves, their degenerate descendants. The vast ages were simply a way of showing this. It was not a Jewish invention, it was normal in the Near East. With Abraham we enter history and he is down to a comparatively meager two hundred years old.

"Saul has slain his thousands and David his tens of thousands" meant that David not Saul had slain Goliath.

One time Christ says that we should forgive unto seventy times seven ("and not once more, saith the Lord," as I heard a lady shout at an outdoor meeting). Another time he phrases it "seven times a day." The number is not the point. Both are ways of saying we should forgive always.

It is part of a different attitude to numbers that their use of "many" and "all" confuses us. "Many are called but few are chosen" need have meant no more than that all are called but fewer, i.e., not all, are chosen.

When Christ at the Last Supper speaks of his blood "poured out for many for the forgiveness of sins," Paul quite normally speaks of God giving up his Son *for us all.*

b) Hyperbole, the use of exaggeration as a way of ensuring that the listeners should not only get the point but remember it, exists in our writing, but to nothing like the same extent.

To his own misfortune Origen took literally the phrase about "some who have made themselves eunuchs for the sake of the Kingdom of Heaven." He came to realize that it was only a rather emphatic way of speaking of celibacy chosen for the service of God.

c) "I have come not to bring peace but a sword": with us this would mean that the sword was the purpose of his coming; for them it meant that it would be a result of his coming. Where with us "to" and "that" normally mean "in order that," with them they could equally well mean "with the result that."

d) Chronology rode them more lightly. If they are telling something Christ said or did, and they remember some related thing said or done at another time, they simply put it in, not bothering to tell us of the time gap. Scholars, for instance, seem agreed that some of the phrases in the Sermon on the Mount are brought in from other occasions. There is no evidence that chapters 15-17 of John were spoken by Christ not at the Last Supper but after the Resurrection. Still they might have been, and we get fresh light by reading them occasionally as if they had been.

2.

There is a vaster difference, not in their way of writing but in our way of reading. The Gospels were written for people who could read. The multiplication of books by printing was fourteen hundred years away in the future, so that most people could not read at all. But those who could, really could, precisely because books were so scarce. When they got a book it might be years before they got another. So they really read that one. The writer could write short books, he did not need to say everything: if something was implied by what he said, there was no point in his spelling it out: the reader could be relied on to get it for himself, he had all the time in the world. We, spoon-fed, must learn a different reading habit. We must read slowly, living it as we read it.

We should imagine ourselves present at every scene. Every so often through my life I have heard the parable of the Pharisee and the publican preached on: not once have I heard the congregation reminded that one of the Twelve, Matthew, had been a tax-extorter himself: it brings a very vivid element into our picture.

If we did develop the habit of reading as if we were present, we should not find ourselves wondering what to say when some nondevotee of Our Lady challenges us with "Jesus never called her mother." We could remind him that only three sentences are recorded as spoken by him to her, so that the absence of the word mother means no lack of filial feeling! To test the questioner's Gospel knowledge we might add that Christ is never addressed as Jesus by any of his followers, and only three times by anyone.

CHAPTER THREE

What Do We Know of Christ?

1.

From the opening of the Apostles' Creed, most Christians remember that Jesus Christ was the only Son of God the Father, that he was conceived by the power of the Holy Spirit, and born of a virgin, Mary. So he was a man, but there was divinity in him. These facts about him we have been uttering all our lives.

But it would be hard to find anywhere a score of words in which so much is concentrated. Normally we break down sentences into their component words; here we must break down every word into its component sentences, and these again into their component volumes. What are the words saying? In all eternity we shall not have exhausted that. What are they saying *to us here and now?* We can at least make a beginning.

"A man with divinity in him." We have found a handy formula for that, God-man. And splendid it is. It contains both elements. But it gives no information as to *how* creator and creature could possibly be combined in one person, or *what* their combination can possibly issue in. The *how* has exercised the minds of thinkers inside the Church and outside from the beginning. The *what* is Jesus Christ, portrayed in the four Gospels.

Since we must begin our exploration of him some-where, I choose what two of his most notable followers said of him. He was the fruit of David's loins, Peter told the crowd after Pentecost (Acts 2:30). He was of the seed of David according to the flesh, so Paul phrased it more technically for the Romans (1:3). From both we learn the same thing—that Son of God though he was, he was not given a body fresh-minted for him: he got it from a myriad ancestors. There were forty generations in the direct male line back to King David, through Bathsheba—David had got rid of her husband in one of the foulest of those slayings which stain the Old Testament's pages.

From all eternity he was Son of God the Father (John 1:11-14). Toward the end of the reign of Palestine's excep-tionally homicidal ruler, King Herod, who died in 4 B.C., he was made man—conceived virginally by Mary, a car-penter's wife. Luke's Gospel speaks of her as "betrothed" to Joseph, but this word is an effort to express an element in Jewish marriage law which has no equivalent among ourselves—in a brief ritual a Jewish couple became man and wife: then the wife returned to her parents' home to be trained for her new role: at the end of a year, the man brought her to his own house: there the marriage feast took place (as at Cana, John 2:1).

But during that year they really were husband and wife; they were not supposed to have bodily union, but if they did and a child was born the child was legitimate. It was in this between period that Jesus was conceived, as the angel had announced:

The Holy Spirit will come upon you
And the power of the Most High will overshadow you,

Therefore the child to be born of you will be called holy
 The Son of God.

After the wedding Jesus was born in Bethlehem.

He had a complete human nature—a soul created, as
yours and mine were, direct by God; a body coming to
him through his Mother from ancestors beyond counting.
He was not simply man, he was that man. By his genes he
had aptitudes and in-aptitudes, things he found attractive
and things he found repellent. "He was tempted in all
things as we are, but did not sin" (Heb. 4:15).

Nothing was handed him on a plate. In coping with life
he never used his divinity, his Sonship of God, to enable
him to sidestep any of life's difficulties. He had to grow
up, for instance. Schooldays would have been as painful
for him as for most boys, the scourging by Pilate would not
have been his first.

Of his first thirty years or so we have one single
episode—when he was twelve he left his parents and was
found by them in the Temple (Luke 2:46). After that he
returned to Nazareth and was an obedient son to Joseph
and Mary: "He grew in wisdom and in stature and in favor
with God and men." Clearly, there was no display of
supernormality in those years—when he returned famous
to Nazareth they could hardly believe it—"Isn't this the
carpenter's son . . .?"

Naturally, we are tempted to speculate about him—
how much did he know and how soon, that he had a
special relation to the Father? To the Holy Spirit? His
growth in wisdom would have had some bearing on that.
It would have some bearing too on the age at which Mary

and Joseph might have decided to tell him as much as they themselves knew—that Mary was his mother, that he had no human father, what the angel had told Mary, what had been revealed to Joseph—"That which is conceived in Mary your wife is of the Holy Spirit: she will bear a son, and you shall call his name Jesus, for he will save his people from their sins" (Matt. 1:21).

All this involves Father, Son, and Holy Spirit: how much did any of the three in the carpenter's shop know of the Trinity? It is not in the Old Testament. By his divinity the boy would have been omniscient, but did that blaze through, or seep through, to his humanity? The human mind can know the fact of the Trinity only if God reveals it. But we are not told how or when God revealed it to the human mind of Jesus. Or what it meant to him when God did. Our human minds find it difficult to comprehend what it means that Christ was a God-man; did his human mind find it much easier to comprehend what it meant to be one?

Speculation about all this is attractive, provided we know that it is only speculation. We can have no experience of our own to give us any more than likelihood as to how a God-man would respond to given situations. The only authority on Christ is Christ—what he says of himself, which is very little; what we see him doing.

He grew in wisdom, which includes self-knowledge. As we grow in manhood, he grew in God-manhood. But apart from the incident in the Temple when he was twelve, his growing is not under our gaze. We are shown only the twenty-six months of his life from his baptism by John to Calvary. (We arrive at twenty-six months by following the Jewish feasts to which John attaches various occurrences. It has been suggested that some of these feasts may have been in different years. If so, we don't know how long the public life lasted.)

In the beginning of those very public months we find a revealing link with his boyhood. His Mother had said in the Temple, "Your father and I have sought you sorrowing"—by Jewish custom Joseph, having accepted him and presented him in the Temple, was his father. The boy answered by claiming a mightier fatherhood— "Didn't you know that I must be in my Father's house" (Luke 2:50). At the baptism in Jordan, twenty years or so later, the Father acknowledged the boy's claim, "This is my beloved Son, in whom I am well pleased" (Matt. 3:17). A great deal is written about the effect on him of this public acknowledgment by his Father. Remember when reading it, that this is our first meeting with Jesus grown up. We have no information at all as to what he thought, felt, feared, hoped before it. But I think we may see one effect on him of his being acknowledged as Son, when in teaching us to pray he could invite us to call his Father ours.

2.

What was he like to meet? The one quality in him generally agreed upon is his loving kindness. Supposing we had to describe him for an unbelieving friend, the chances are we should begin with that. But the other would naturally want illustrations. After all, so many religious founders have been kind and loving. Pause upon what you would say. That he said, "Love your neighbor as yourself" (Matt. 22:39)? But that is a quotation from the Old Testament. That he said, "Suffer little children to come unto me and forbid them not" (Mark 10:14)? Excellent, your listener might agree: but if you finished the quotation—"for of such is the Kingdom of Heaven," he might be puzzled; if he had been having trouble with his own children, quarreling among themselves and driving their mother to the verge of insanity, he might want to know why children should be the ideal citizens of the Kingdom of Heaven. You might have to ask for notice of that question, unless you had already given the deep thought to it that any word of the God-man demands. Paul makes it clear that while we enter as children, we must put away the things of a child and grow up (1 Cor. 13:11).

Certainly, some people who knew Christ in his lifetime would have been startled to find so much made of his loving kindness, indeed might have wondered if you were talking of the same person.

There were the Pharisees to whom he said, "The harlots and tax-exploiters will enter the Kingdom of Heaven before you" (Matt. 21:31); whom he had compared with tombs, "all whitewashed on the outside, but inside full of dead men's bones and all filthiness" (Matt. 23:27). For sustained invective it would be hard to match anywhere in the world's literature his portrait of them in Matthew's chapter 23.

There were the money-changers whom he drove out of a court of the Temple because they were making his Father's house a den of thieves. These people, we feel, deserved all they got from tongue and whip—they had

desecrated God's house, as the hypocrites among the
Pharisees desecrated God's image in man.

But there were individuals too. The Gentile woman
who had asked him to heal her daughter (Mark 7:25) must
have felt his "Do you want me to take the bread of the
children and give it to dogs?" as an assertion of her in-
feriority as a Gentile: he did heal her daughter, and that
was kindness to the limit of her hopes; but did she feel him
loving?

Even the Apostles—whom "he loved, and to the end"
(John 13:1)—would not forget his "Have you no sense, no
wits, are your hearts dulled, can't your eyes see, your ears
hear, don't you remember?" (Mark 6:51). Peter surely
would never have forgotten the shock of Christ's "Get
behind me, Satan, you are a stumbling block to me; for
you are not on the side of God but of men."

John, to whose first Epistle we owe the glory of the
phrase "God is love," had met the hard firmness three
times: when he and his brother asked for high places in
Christ's kingdom, his ambition was tossed back on him so
decisively (Mark 10:38); when he wanted fire from heaven
to consume a Samaritan city which would not receive
Christ, he was rebuked, "You do not know what manner
of spirit you are, for the Son of man came not to destroy
men's lives but to save them" (Luke 9:56); when he asked
how Peter was to die he was told in effect to mind his own
business (John 21:22).

Jesus was simply not given to sentimental utterance.
We are told, by the Evangelists not by himself, of a
handful of people he loved—the Apostles, as we have just
seen; the unnamed one of them "that he loved" (John

12:23); the rich young man who left Jesus because he could not face selling his "great possessions" and giving the money to the poor; Lazarus and the family at Bethany. That is the whole list.

The list of people he praised is if anything even shorter—there is a centurion, "I have not found such faith in Israel" (Luke 7:9); a scribe, "You are not far from the Kingdom of God" (Mark 12:34); John the Baptist, "among those born of women there has arisen none greater than he"—high praise, but followed by "he who is least in the Kingdom of Heaven is greater" (Matt. 11:11); Nathanael, "an Israelite without guile"—not very exuberant, you might think, but significant as the first quality he praised in one of the Apostles: the men who were to succeed them in the Church do not all seem to have possessed it.

There is plenty of emotion in him—for example, his anger and grief at those who accused him of breaking the Sabbath when he healed the man with a withered hand (Mark 3:5). But we do not need all the fingers of one hand to count the times he showed any of the gentler emotions—twice he wept (over Jerusalem and over dead Lazarus); once he was joyful (not to know why is to miss something very important in him—read it in Luke 10, Matthew 11). We never see him smile at all.

With individuals he was very much the doctor with a duty not only to tell them what was wrong with them, but to make sure they realized it. On the multitude, however, "he had compassion, for they were helpless and harassed like sheep without a shepherd." Yet one wonders how much he showed it: for they too had to have the truth.

His settled habit was terseness of speech. When his

Mother told him of her sorrow and Joseph's at his having deserted them for three days his answer began, "Didn't you know—" then he went home "and was obedient to them." When she suggested a miracle at Cana, his words were, "What has it got to do with us?"—then he worked the miracle.

The living element in his whole being is his love for his Father. But we hear him say it once only (John 14:31): "I do as the Father has commanded me, so that the world may know that I love the Father." Having said it, he goes out to Gethsemane and death.

Reading over these last pages, I see why some of my friends find him not very attractive. He seems not to have spread himself to win affection. Yet he did, in his lifetime, draw people to him: again something in the personality must have given the bluntness of his words a different feel. And this comes through in the Gospel pages, now as all down all the centuries.

3.

Christ Jesus was man unmistakable. But hardly man typical. Throughout his public life he affirmed that he was different—not by shouting it but by doing and saying, with all naturalness, things that would have been either monstrous or ridiculous in any other man. Think of a carpenter saying to a fisherman—"I will give you the keys of the Kingdom of Heaven."

We, reading the Sermon on the Mount, can take it in our stride, with no awareness of the shock he gave the Jewish crowd, hearing them new, by statements like,

"Don't think I have come to abolish the Law and the Prophets." To his hearers it was much as it would be to us if a young carpenter we had never heard of said for our reassurance that he did not mean to abolish the American Constitution. We would almost certainly laugh it off—but no one ever seems to have been able to do that with Jesus. If we took it seriously, our only possible reaction would be, "Who does he think he is?" Later (Matt. 16:13), he would ask his followers who *they* thought he was, to be answered by Peter with, "You are the Christ, the Son of the living God." It may have won him the papacy—and, quoted by the high priest to the Sanhedrin, it assured Christ's Crucifixion and our redemption. (Matt. 26:62).

But the original reaction stood then, as it stands now—who *did* he think he was? He was forever tantalizing his hearers. Later in the Sermon he takes three of the Commandments—you shall not kill, commit adultery, bear false witness—and proceeds to develop them by going to their very roots. He introduces each of the three with the words, "It was said to them of old"—by God through Moses!—"but I say unto you." Once again there could only be a shocked "Who does he think he is?" From the beginning there must have been many who thought him mad, as we find some of his relatives doing—"They went out to seize him, for they said 'He is beside himself' " (Mark 3:10). Words like, "If you shall love father or mother more than me you are not worthy of me" (Matt. 10:37) would suggest megalomania if he were man and nothing more.

One could, I suppose, be content to take each shock as it comes, wince a little, then just go on swallowing whatever he said or did. This roughly is what the Apostles did when the crowd was leaving him after his announcement that if we are to have life in us we must eat his flesh and drink his blood (John 6:52). Indeed, we feel as our own Peter's question, "To whom should we go?" Who else is there? But that would be no way to accept anyone. We must follow Peter to the end of his sentence, "You have the words of eternal life." Yet those words do not carry their meaning clear on their face: we must grow into them.

The Apostles *had* to wonder first what he was, but sooner or later with a kind of panic, *who* he could possibly be. One advantage of the Gospels is that they enable us to live with the Apostles as they moved toward certainty. Was he the Christ, the Messiah (both words, one Greek, the other Hebrew, mean "anointed") of Israel? Was he human or divine? We can hardly blame them for not seeing instantly that he might be both.

We shall gain a lot if we make the effort to live their bewilderment with them. He did not begin by giving them the answers and then proceed to lecture them on God-manhood and redemption. They had to grow into both, as they made what they could of such a variety of things he said and did, forcing his audiences to feel that he was at least claiming something unique.

The phrase "Son of man," for instance. We meet it in the Gospels used of himself by Christ (and by no one else) some fifty times. The phrase was simply a solemn way of saying "man"—a good hundred times God had addressed the prophet Ezekiel so. Christ's use of it answered no questions, merely showed that there *was* a question.

In Luke (chapter 10) and Matthew (chapter 11) we have the first explicit statement he made of his divinity. After the return of the seventy-two disciples, he says to them: "No one knows the Son except the Father, and no one knows the Father except the Son and anyone to whom the Son chooses to reveal him": he asserts a uniqueness of interknowledge between himself and God the Father: and he is not clutching his privilege to himself but has come to share it with men.

The way was ready for Peter's "You are the Christ, the Son of the living God." How much did Peter realize of what he was saying? Less, certainly, than when he told the crowd on Pentecost day, "You killed the author of life." By then Calvary and the Resurrection had happened; he had heard Thomas say to Christ, "My Lord and my God."

When Peter called Christ "the Son of the living God," he was not following the tradition by which men who held a special function in Israel—priests, judges—were called sons of God. That would not have caused Christ to say, "Flesh and blood has not revealed it to you but my Father who is in heaven"; nor would it have caused the high priest (to whom an informer, Judas perhaps, had reported it) to make it the key question in the charge of blasphemy (Mark 14:61). But how did Peter think that God could have a son? Christ had said that he is a spirit; the whole Old Testament saw him as wholly free of sex, in which all the pagan gods indulged maniacally.

In Acts and Epistles Christ's divinity was asserted again and again without the question apparently arising. Only in the first words of John's Gospel do we find the key: "In the beginning was the Word, and the Word was with God, and the Word was God. He was in the beginning with God; all things were made through him. . . . And the Word became flesh and dwelt among us, full of grace and truth; we have beheld his glory, glory as of the only Son from the Father."

The word "Word" is strange here. The Greek word is *Logos* and scholars have made much of its use by the Alexandrian Jew Philo in a different sense—Philo could not conceivably have said that his *Logos* "became flesh and dwelt among us." We need no great scholarship to notice that by verse 14 "Word" has become "Son," and Son it is for the rest of the Gospel.

Why did John use it at all, since he meant to make no further use of it? Look carefully at the opening we have just read. A word uttered by a pure spirit could not be a sound issuing from the lungs and shaped by tongue and teeth and lips! It could be only a spiritual uttering, a thought, a concept, an idea. So God had an Idea, with him from the beginning, i.e., from all eternity; *and this Idea was God.* The main line of Christian thinking has held that the only idea which could possibly *be* God is God's Idea of himself. The Word then is God's Idea of himself uttered eternally within himself.

The notion of having an idea of oneself is a good entry-way for us. We all have one. And merely to compare what ours is with what the Father's must be casts light for us.

We know that our idea of ourself is not very adequate —it leaves out too much that our friends find in us; it constantly runs into the shock of surprise that we are worse than we thought. But the Father's Idea can be only of total adequacy: what would be the point of one who already knows himself perfectly conceiving, bringing into eternal existence, an inadequate Idea of himself?

The Second Person, the Word, lacks nothing of the Father's own fullness of being, "God from God, light from light"—all-powerful, all-knowing, all-loving. So we have two Persons, two selves, within the one Godhead, each God, yet not two Gods, since the very existence of the Second consists in being "thought" by the First.

Thus both Word and Son express likeness. A son is always of the nature of his father; the whole point of an idea is its likeness to that which it is an idea *of*. But the Idea, wholly spiritual, does not raise the sort of questions about fatherhood in God which we have seen raised by Son. That, conceivably, is why John began his Gospel with it.

Two persons within the Oneness of God must have meant as great a strain on a group of Jews as the earlier statement that salvation involved eating Christ's flesh and drinking his blood. But whereas the latter had Peter asking, "To whom else shall we go?" his divinity had them bewildered indeed but genuinely using their minds.

The same with the introduction by Christ of a Third—the Holy Spirit. It was St. Augustine's great insight, accepted throughout the Western Church, that just as the Second Person issues from the First by way of Knowledge, the Third, the Spirit, proceeds from the First and Second by way of Love.

Return for a moment to our idea of ourself. We might admire it, even like it; but we cannot imagine it as admiring us, liking us. For it is only something, not someone. But the Father's Idea of himself *is* Someone, and can love as he is loved. Father and Son unite in a love which fills the whole divine nature, giving it all they have, so there is now a Third Person within the divine Oneness, equal to them in all perfections, God as they are God. But not a third God, for he exists in virtue of the Love of Father and Son which produces him. It may be mere fancy that we see a fitness in his very name. In Hebrew, as in Greek and Latin, the root meaning of spirit is "breath." It is pleasant to think of Father and Son breathing forth their love.

It is the Second Person who became man, took human nature, and made it as wholly his own as your nature is yours, mine, mine. When we say that Christ is God we are not saying that he is Trinity: it is a kind of shorthand for the truth that the person, that in him which said I, was, is, the Trinity's Second Person.

This is part of that main line of Christian thinking which I have just mentioned. It was hammered out through Council after Council over five centuries. That one of the three became man and the others did not is a reminder that while each is wholly God, yet each is wholly himself. It is not a case of a top copy and two carbons!

Another reminder of the same truth is that while in relation to us and to all creation the Trinity acts as One, we are encouraged to associate ("appropriate" is the technical word) certain actions especially with one or another of them. Thus the First Person, being Origin and Power, we see as Creator. Yet John and Paul both speak of all things as created *through* the Second—who within the Godhead exists by way of Intelligence. In other words, Omnipotence produces something from nothing, Intelligence makes it an ordered something. Then the Third Person, existing by way of Love, comes into the front of the picture, to give men the gifts they need.

When the order was broken by sin, the same Second Person became man to make the new order. With the new order made, the Third comes to the front again, to give men the gifts the new order calls for.

You may feel more darkness in all this than light, but light there is—if we persist.

Postscript on Theological Terms

For one wholly new to this kind of reading, the terms person and nature need thinking about. The doctrine of the Trinity is expressed as Three Persons in one God, or Three Persons in one divine nature. Christ himself we see as one Person with two natures, divine and human.

Nature answers the question, What is it? In a rational nature person answers the question, Who is it? If a room is dark and we are aware that there is some object there, we ask what it is. If it is clearly a human being, we ask who it is.

Again, nature, what the thing is, decides what it can do and what can be done with it and to it. But nature does not do the things or suffer them—the person does all that.

Applying this crudely, but I hope clearly enough, to our two doctrines—

If you asked the Three who they were, one would answer "the Father," one would answer "the Son," one would answer "the Spirit." If you asked them, "What are you"—there would be one answer, "God," for each wholly possesses the divine nature and can do all that goes with being God.

If you asked Christ who he was, the answer would be, "God the Son." If one asked what he was, the answer would be, "I am God, I am man."

Enough of these improbable conversations. A simpler definition of person is "That which can say I." Apply this to Christ and we find "I" used on two levels—"I and the Father are one." "I thirst." God the Son speaks in the nature which is his eternally from the Father, and in the nature which became his in the womb of Mary. The student will find a dozen clarifications needed, for God is not a diagram, neither is Christ. But, with all their crudity, these bits and pieces may help beginners.

PART TWO
The Difference to Us

CHAPTER FOUR

What Life
Is All About

1.

We began with the question what it matters to us that Christ lived and died and rose again. What have we gained by his life, his death, his Resurrection? What should we have lost if he had not lived, not died, not risen?

All the reality involved in the answers to these questions we shall not know till we have reached maturity in heaven. But a careful study of what he has told us on all three makes for our adulthood, not only as members of Christ, which we are, but as citizens of the world, which also we are. Both Church and world gain by our adulthood.

One need not be a believer to see that if he had not lived we should have lost a heroic example of courage and sacrifice. Merely as a myth, his story would give us the sense of a possibility worth living toward.

Even if we found "Love your enemies, do good to them that hate you" just too unrealistic, we could see its nobility as an ideal, could see indeed all the good that might come of it if only it were possible. As not myth but reality, uttered by one who, while nailed to a cross, said of his torturers, "Father forgive them, for they know not what they do," it has led vast numbers through the centuries to see not only its possibility but its practicality, and so to live by it, to die by it.

For Christ was not thinking out copybook maxims; he was stating, with clinical precision, the facts of life. Among them he gave us the most elementary fact of all—the framework of reality with the human race in it; and he answered the most elementary of all questions—what is life all about?

Life on earth is a road not a dwelling place. We are all going, not staying. Going where? What follows death?

"That," a young logical positivist said to me in Aberdeen, "is a nonquestion." "Maybe," I answered, "but I still want to know." That millions of people should be on a road, never asking why they are on it or where it leads, concerned only with making the journey more agreeable, passes my understanding. Some of them devote their lives to the wellbeing of other travelers: they are wonderful people but their unselfishness does not compensate for the defect in the mind which causes them not even to see that the questions *are* questions, the answers essential if life is to be lived *and people helped* intelligently.

When I speak of defect in the mind I am not implying that people are mentally deficient who take the road of life as it is and just go on from there. Plenty of men to whom the questions never seem to have occurred are more mentally muscular than I am. But certainly on this basic matter their minds are not functioning.

Neither the scientist *as* scientist, nor the philosopher *as* philosopher, can help us on the first question. Each of them can do marvels with what he finds already in existence. But how it came to be there, why anything at all exists, and to what purpose—Kant's question, "Why isn't there nothing?"—neither of them can answer. And that question left unanswered puts a question mark against all they think they do know.

The scientist and the philosopher, like you and me and everybody else, can know the answer only if they are told. Christ has told us.

To be on a road and not know why one is on it or where it leads is to be lost. Christ had "come to seek and to save that which is lost" (Luke 19:10).

There is more than one way of being lost, more than one kind of lostness. He had used those particular words about a tax-extorter, lost morally. But all lostness was Christ's affair, and he had a special concern for those who have lost their way. One of his best-known utterances is, "I am the Way, and the Truth, and the Life" (John 14:6). He said this at the Last Supper in answer to a question asked by the Apostle Thomas.

Christ is the Way. The way to what? That also he answered, "No man comes to the Father but by me." So he himself is not the goal, the Father is. Having found him we have found the Way, which does not mean that we have found salvation—we might still wander from the Way by error, might still fall by the wayside for want of the energy to make the efforts and resistances that walking the Way calls for. As against error, we need truth; as against failure of energy, we need life. And Christ is both.

"I have come to bear witness to the truth."

"I am come that you may have life and have it more abundantly."

He is Revealer and Redeemer, truth-bearer, life-bearer. As both, Christ is in eclipse. As both, we shall look closely at him. It is the most practically useful thing we can do. Self-interest says that we should give it urgent priority. The trouble is the world seems to offer self so much that is more immediately and more obviously interesting.

2.

To repeat: we cannot live our lives intelligently if we don't know what life is about: which breaks down into how we happen to exist, indeed how anything at all exists, and where (if anywhere) we are supposed to be going. Not knowing the answers, we can only stumble and fumble, splendidly or idiotically or with idiocy and splendor interwoven, in each one's inimitable, individual style.

Christ's answer to why and whither can be summarized—God at our beginning, God our goal. God is Alpha and Omega, the first letter of the Greek alphabet and the last—as it might be A and Z. God creates us out of nothing, that we may come to fullness of being in direct union with him at the end, which is our true beginning and will have no end.

For the origin of all things, Christ, as we shall see in a moment, gives his own endorsement to the first three chapters of Genesis. Chapter 1, written after chapters 2 and 3, gives us the hymn of creation—One God causing the universe to exist by his sole will, bringing humanity into it at the very end of the process, male and female made in his image.

For the human race and what happened to it in its origin, chapters 2 and 3 give the story. The writer did not know the detail—the when or the where or the exactly how, but he knew from God the essential of it, all in it that affects us. He tells it as the story of a man and woman in a garden, and of a sin committed by them: but the garden is the world, the man is Everyman, the woman is Everywoman, the sin is Everysin. He faced the double question why God, all-holy, all-living, should have produced a universe in which the highest beings find sin irresistible and death unavoidable. Either by revelation or by his own God-aided meditation he saw that death must be linked with sin, and that sin could only have arisen from man's desire to be his own God. Christ gives his endorsement by quoting its words, "They shall be two in one flesh" (Gen. 2:24), telling us that the words are God's (whose they are Genesis leaves unclear), making them the basis of his own teaching on marriage.

So at the origin of the universe and at man's origin in it, there was a mind. Had there been no mind the universe would have been an accident which happened to happen, and man a byproduct of the accident—with no meaning and no purpose, for there would have been no mind to mean him or have a design for him. All would exist in a context of meaninglessness, and meaninglessness would have the last word—the last word on men, certainly, billions of them emerging unmeant from an unmeant universe and doomed in their billions to sink back into it. It is hard to see what value such a being could have; we might still tell ourselves that all men are equal, but we should have to admit that if so they are all equal to nothing much.

To the whole human race and not only its religious section, it is of measureless importance to have been "meant" and not merely to have happened. Nothing could do more for human relations than to take for a fact of life that every man is made by God in his own image, and so is of value simply as a man. It is not easy for us to see this, because of the mess we have all made of ourselves by our sins and the mess other men have made of us by their injustices. But if we had the basic fact built into our awareness, every instinct would make us want to heal the mess—in ourselves, in others—rather than to enjoy it in ourselves and exploit it in others.

3.

Since God means so much, not only in himself, but to us, it would be strange not to want to know him better. Here is a first summarizing of things Christ tells us about him: he is the one only God, to be loved with all the power of mind and heart (Mark 12:44). He is good; he and he only is goodness in its plenitude (Matt. 19:17). He is perfect (Matt. 5:48). All things are possible to him, even the salvation of the rich—that being the example Christ himself gives (Matt. 19:26). He is hidden, dwells in secret. Of God, Christ uses only one noun; God is a spirit, he tells the Samaritan woman at the well (John 4:24). We have known the phrase all our lives. It is not to be found in the Old Testament.

God is concerned with, involved with, the world he made. Christ shows him seeing, hearing, listening, answering, caring, loving, merciful, rewarding, punishing, forgiving (provided men forgive), condemning their heartlessness, giving himself, withdrawing himself from those who refuse him. He clothes the grasses of the field. No sparrow falls without his knowledge.

There is nothing here to surprise a Jew who knew his Bible. This is not the multitudinous god of the pagans. Still less is it the impersonal absolute of Hindus and Buddhists, brought by Plotinus a couple of centuries after Christ into a Europe prepared for it by Aristotle and Plato. Many Christian leaders today have been captivated by the notion, some of them in our own Church. They would agree that neither the prophets of Israel nor Christ himself knew such a deity. It is hard to see what fascination they find in a faceless, featureless being, what light he can bring into our darkness, what strength to our impotence.

Aristotle and Plato and Plotinus were men of immense spiritual genius but they knew nothing of Calvary, and had not received Christ eucharistically as we have; they had heard of groups of three among the gods of paganism, but none of these bear any resemblance to the Oneness of the Trinity.

With the revelation of a Son and a Holy Spirit within the unity of the Godhead, not breaking the unity but enriching it, Christ takes us where no pagan had gone, no Jew either—into the inner life of God.

We have already seen that it was after rejoicing in the Holy Spirit because his Father had given the seventy-two disciples insights "hidden from the wise and perfect" of Israel, that Christ made the first explicit statement of a plurality within the divine Oneness. "All things have been delivered to me by my Father. And no one knows the Son but the Father, and no one knows the Father but the Son." Do reread Luke 10:17-24 carefully.

How, we may wonder, does the inner life of God concern us?

The immediate answer is that to our coming into existence and remaining in existence we have contributed nothing: we owe both to the will of God. The character of one in whose hands we so wholly are *must* concern us. A god totally indifferent to us, or a god to whom nothing matters but his own majesty, would make life wholly other, bleakly other, frighteningly other.

There is no more certain proof of love than the desire to know and be known. One might serve another in myriad ways—from sympathy or pity or sense of duty. But only where there is love is there a desire to know and to be known. Christ has said, "Greater love no man has than willingness to die for a friend." As man he gave that proof of love, he laid down his life for us. But as God the Son he gave this other proof, he laid open God's life to us. He not only loves us, he wants our love.

He not only wants our love. He wants us. Paul says (1 Cor. 13), "If a man gave his body to be burned and has not love it profits him nothing." And a verse or two later he makes the link between loving and knowing—in God's plan we are to know God as he knows us. This knowing comes to perfection in heaven, but its root is here.

God's love itself finds new depth in the Trinity. The Old Testament God was indeed a loving God. But whom does an infinite God love? Us? Yes, thank God. But we are poor objects of infinite love, we cannot comprehend it, we cannot return it. Must God always be loving beneath him? Within the Trinity our question is answered. Within the Godhead there is an eternal interflow of life and knowledge and love among Father, Son, and Holy Spirit. The God of Israel was loving. But only the revelation of the Trinity makes possible the crowning phrase of all religion—God is love. It is John who says it, in his first Epistle (1 John 4:8). There is no question from whom he got it.

Why are we here? Where are we supposed to be going? We have seen Christ's answers—our origin and our goal. But how do we get there? To answer that Christ came into our world. The rest of the book is about his answer.

CHAPTER FIVE

What Christ Had Come For

A few days before his death on Calvary, Our Lord knew fear—"Father save me from this hour" (John 12:27). He recovered instantly—"Yet for this hour I have come." That is, he had come to die.

In the twenty-six months from Cana to Calvary, twenty-six months in which he is under our gaze, he lived in the shadow of death, marching steadily toward it: which may be why we never see him smile. As the crisis approaches, Matthew, Mark, and Luke show him telling the Apostles of it more than once. But John has him telling Nicodemus earlier: "As Moses lifted up the serpent in the wilderness, so must the Son of man be lifted up, that whoever believes in him may have eternal life" (3:14).

He was referring to the brazen figure of a serpent erected by Moses at God's command to save the Israelites from a desert plague of poisonous snakes (Num. 21:8): Christ saw himself lifted up for the salvation of the people, under a death threat from a mightier foe. I have read, but cannot remember where, that "lifted up" was a colloquial phrase for crucifixion. Whether it was or not, when Christ says, "If I be lifted up I will draw all men to me," John adds the comment, "He was referring to the death he was to die" (John 12:32). So his mind was on his death not long after Cana, and a few days before Calvary, with another reference to "lifting up" in between (John 8:28).

Why was he so sure he was to be slain? Why was he so sure that this was what he had come for? Clearly there was something specific in what he had come into our race to do, which accounted for both certainties. Consider other things he says about why he had come:

"To bear witness to the truth" (John 18:37).

"To preach the Gospel of the Kingdom" (Matt. 4:23).

This, as we shall see, was the element in his mission which caused not only bad men to want him dead, but even men of genuine devotion to see him as a threat to all that Israel meant to them: bad men and good united for his slaying.

Listen again:

"To seek and to save that which was lost" (Luke 19:10).

"Not to bring the just but sinners to repentance" (Luke 5:32).

This accent on sin fits with what Joseph was told in a dream—"He shall be called Jesus, because he shall save his people from their sins" (Matt. 1:21). And this may be the element in his mission which he saw he would best accomplish by giving up his life.

Consider the elements separately.

1.

Anyone who talks of a kingdom to be established will sooner or later run into trouble with the Establishment already there. In Judea that meant the Roman procurator, Pontius Pilate; in Galilee it meant Herod Antipas, ruling by Caesar's permission and wholly under his thumb.

Hand in glove with the Roman power were the Sadducees who had the Temple and the high priesthood: in Christ's lifetime Rome appointed to the position Annas, followed by five of his sons and a son-in-law—this one was Caiaphas who handed Christ over to Pilate and jockeyed Pilate into having him crucified.

This union of Church and State was the official Establishment. But there was an unofficial establishment too. The Sadducees had the Temple in Jerusalem, where alone sacrifice could be offered. But the Pharisees dominated the synagogues all over Palestine and indeed wherever Jews gathered in the great world outside.

The Sadducees were rich, a small minority therefore. The Pharisees were men of strict observance, they, too, therefore a small minority. The mass of Jews had no more devotion to the Sadducees than the mass of people anywhere have to the rich. The Pharisees were not rich, though there were rich men among them: they were admired, and indeed revered, for the minuteness of their study of the Scriptures and their rigorous observance of the Law down to its smallest details. The main religious difference between the two groups lay in what they regarded as Scripture.

The Sadducees held themselves bound only by the five books of Moses, read in all literalness: they did not believe in survival after death, for instance, because they could not find it in the five books of Moses. The Pharisees saw these as of supreme authority, but they also regarded the historical and prophetical books and the Psalms as true Scripture: they held that God's last word to his people had not been uttered in the desert thirteen hundred years before. Most of the scribes, men who gave their whole lives to the study of the Bible, seem to have been Pharisees. Most of the members of the Sanhedrin, the Supreme Council of the Jews, were Sadducees.

The Sadducees, of course, had no devotion to the foreign conquerors; but they had decided to work in with them while they were there; perhaps one day they would go. But it was themselves who went. Forty years or so after Christ's death the Romans destroyed Jerusalem, the Sadducees vanished from history. It was the Pharisees who were to be the living, guiding element in Judaism.

The talk of a kingdom had begun with John the Baptist. It must have been a relief to Pharisees and Sadducees, whom he had called to their faces a brood of vipers, when Herod's sword took his head off.

If so, their relief did not last long. The forerunner had made them uneasy but the one he foreran was immeasurably worse.

Strangely, considering the preaching of a kingdom, the political establishment was the last to show awareness of him. Even its religious wing, the high priests, did not swing immediately into action. It was "the scribes and Pharisees" who pursued him from the beginning of the twenty-six months.

Why? Not for the attacks on themselves, I think, scattered over the Gospels and concentrated in Matthew's twenty-third chapter. The best of them, men like Gamaliel, would have agreed: a little later their own writers would scourge them in the same terms: and a little after that St. John Chrysostom would find Catholics just as bad—"We imitate the hypocrites, we even surpass them."

The most religious of the Pharisees could see Christ only as threatening so much in Judaism to which they had given themselves heart and soul. What the scribes had done was to analyze the Law syllable by syllable, letter by letter, into such a flood of rules to be observed, six or seven hundred of them, that hardly anyone could observe them all! There were rules about what was permitted to be done on the Sabbath; about washing—after some contacts, before others; about eating—what things could be eaten and with whom—not with nonobservers of the Law, above all not with Gentiles.

All this mass of scribal teaching was known as the traditions and ranked only next to Scripture itself. With no instinct moving them to use their minds upon the nature of God, *what God is,* they studied his attributes as manifested in his actions among men—his love indeed, but his justice ahead of that, and over all his majesty—expressed as power. As Paul was to say of them (Rom. 10:2), "That they are jealous of God's honour I can testify, but it is with imperfect understanding."

It was all very well, they felt, for Christ to say in the Sermon on the Mount, "Think not that I have come to abolish the Law and the Prophets." What else was he doing?

He accused the traditions of contradicting the Law of Moses. To us it may seem a mere statement of the obvious, practically a platitude, to say as he did, "It is not what goes into the mouth that defiles a man but what comes out of the heart" (Matt. 15:11). It was in fact an abolishing of what lay very close to the religion of some of Israel's holiest. The same with his contempt for the ritual washings, his willingness to eat with Gentiles and with the laxest of Jews.

Worse was what he seemed to be claiming for himself—to be able to forgive sins (Matt. 9:6), to be greater than the Temple and to be Lord of the Sabbath (Matt. 12:1-8). It was all leading to the claim to be equal to God, one with the Father, which had them reaching for stones to slay him.

2.

So we see that it was for telling the unwelcome truth that some of the best and worst among the Jewish leaders wanted him slain. But there is our second question—Why was he not only willing to die but convinced that the work he had been sent into the world to do—"for this was I sent"—required his dying? Reflect on how determined he was. Verses 11 to 18 of chapter 10 of St. John's Gospel should be read closely. He is the good shepherd. When robbers come, when wolves come, "The good shepherd lays down his life for his sheep. . . . I lay down my life, that I may take it again. No one takes it from me, I lay it down of my own accord." Realize how closely this concerns us. You and I might read on without remembering that he is talking about you and me. We are the sheep for whom it is his duty to die.

How literally he meant what he said about dying, we find in Matt. 26:51-54. At Jesus' arrest, Peter had swung his sword, and cut off the ear of one of the high priest's servants. Jesus rebuked him, "All who take the sword shall perish by the sword. Do you think that I cannot appeal to my Father and he will send me twelve legions of angels? But if so, how should the Scriptures be fulfilled?"

If we are in that state of pious coma which we have already talked about, we might let our eyes glide right over this—we've read it all before and very impressive it is! How nice that Easter is coming round so that we can read it again.

But if we are awake, two things would set us thinking deeper. It tells of a sudden vast change in Jesus, and it poses a question—what Scriptures demanded that he not avoid whatever was about to happen?

The change: he says that he could have appealed to his Father to save him. But a few verses back he *had* appealed to his Father: "My Father, if it be possible, let this cup pass from me; nevertheless not as I will but as you will": again, "My Father, if this cup cannot pass unless I drink it, your will be done." And again a third time. With the rebuke we have just heard to Peter *and* his "the Scriptures must be fulfilled," we learn that the cup has not passed but that he has been given the strength to drink it. That could be the meaning of the angel sent to strengthen him (Luke 22:44): the older translations read "comfort" but the word means strengthen: certainly, as Luke states it, the angel had brought no comfort—"being in an agony, he prayed more earnestly; and his sweat became like great drops of blood, falling down upon the ground."

Please do not think it impertinent to me to urge readers to give their whole minds to these next few paragraphs.

If we are to know Christ, we cannot miss the strangeness of "Let this cup pass." From the beginning of his public life he had known and spoken of the death he must die. Luke (12:50) tells us of his speaking of the baptism—in his own blood—which awaits him and adds, "How am I constrained until it be accomplished." We have noticed that when Peter urged him not to suffer and die, Christ's response had been, "Get behind me, Satan." We have already wondered if he was asking his Father—three times—for something he had called satanic when Peter first urged it.

The answer lies in the answer to the question —what is this *Scripture that "must be fulfilled"*? If we had read carefully Luke's description of the Last Supper (22:37) we should have known what it was: "I tell you that this Scripture *must be* fulfilled in me—'He was reckoned with the transgressors'; for what is written about me has its fulfilment."

The text he says is being fulfilled in him is one of the most important unnoticed texts in all Scripture. Jesus tells the Apostles, *and us,* the meaning—it practically gives the scenario of what is to happen in the Garden of the Agony and on Calvary. There was no division of Scripture then into chapters and verses. Quoting a text was a way of referring to a whole episode. This text belongs to what we now call the fifty-third chapter of Isaiah. Read it, please. Now!

Here are some of the phrases you will find in it:

He was wounded for our transgressions
He was bruised for our iniquities

Upon him was the chastisement that healed us
And with his stripes we are healed . . .
And the Lord has laid on him the iniquity of us all.

This was not what Peter had been urging him not to undergo (Matt. 16:14). Peter knew nothing of it. What concerned him was Christ's suffering at the hands of the chief priests and scribes followed by the death (the promise of resurrection on the third day seems not to have penetrated!). Had Isaiah, writing this seven or eight hundred years before, been shown what was to happen to Christ? Or, by the suffering servant, did he mean Israel? But he of all people would hardly have thought of Israel as a sinless victim. Was he, perhaps, in light given him by God, seeing what the healing of the world's sin would necessarily demand—very much as the Genesis writer saw what must have been at that sin's origin?

Christ, at any rate, knew that it was about himself.

It was having to bear the burden of all the unrepented sins of mankind that was the new element for Christ. We cannot imagine the physical, psychological, emotional agony of the experience. Neither could Christ till the burden was laid upon him. All we know is that it brought him close to death there in the Garden.

Why was he so determined upon death? What was it he saw that would not be effected unless he was killed? Keep that question steadily in mind in your reading. We shall come to it, as his followers at last did, after living through what actually happened on that night and the day after.

In the last days before Calvary we have seen how he had paid the Establishment, the chief priests and the scribes, with the elders, an insult deeper than which no insult could go—the harlots and tax-extorters would enter the kingdom before them. Nothing, we feel, could have made his death more certain. But he didn't leave it at that. In the parable of the vineyard he told them that they would kill him. The Synoptists (Matt. 21:33, Mark 12:1, Luke 20:9) all have the episode. Read any one of them.

A man planted a vineyard: he sent his servants, whom they variously mistreated, to get his share of the fruit; so the owner decided to send his beloved son. But the tenants "cast him out of the vineyard and killed him."

It was scarcely a parable, this: more like what we should call a *roman à clef*, a story in which the characters are identifiable as living people. The vineyard was Israel, the owner was God, the tenants were themselves. It is all straight out of the fifth chapter of Isaiah. Read that too. Telling the story was rushing on death. We shall meet the same group—"the chief priests, and the scribes and the elders"—at the questioning of Jesus after his arrest, accusing him next day before both Pilate and Herod, mocking him as he hung on the Cross.

CHAPTER SIX

The Sacrifice of Our Redemption

1.

We have just seen what a too casual reading of Luke's account of the Last Supper might have caused us to miss—an element in Gethsemane at once mysterious beyond our imagining and essential to our understanding.

That Christ was suffering and dying for sinful mankind we should in any event have known, having heard it all our lives. We should not have known from how deep within mankind, with how terrible an identification with us in our sinfulness, he worked for our redemption. Our guilt he could not take *in* him, but he took it *on* him. Like everyone else I find it impossible to say in words of one syllable what is contained in the distinction between these two monosyllables.

He could not make his own the guilt of mankind's sins —that was personal to each sinner and not transferable. Nor did the Father make it a condition of forgiving mankind that his Son should be punished *as if* he had committed them himself—that would have meant a monster god saying, "As long as someone gets punished, I'm satisified."

What the man Christ Jesus *could* do was carry to its furthest point an experience not uncommon among men and women—*the experience of suffering to the point of heartbreak because someone they love is behaving callously or treacherously:* their sorrow at the one they love defiling himself matches the sorrow that the person acting evilly ought to be feeling. Something like that, perhaps, was what Isaiah was trying to say. And in the supper room, Christ reminded the Apostles of it, that they might realize the deepest inwardness of what was about to happen.

For Christ loved mankind, loved it even in its sinfulness. Remember how he had grieved over the heartlessness of those who objected to his healing on the Sabbath (Luke 14:14-16). And now that he was to die for sinful mankind he faced what he was dying for. The horror of our sinfulness was laid open to his mind's eye, challenging him to go on loving us. Next day, when they had savaged him to the last ounce of endurance, Pilate would show him to the crowd with the words, *Ecce homo*—Look at the man. But in Gethsemane the man had looked at man!

And not much happened between then and his death to make man's image look any better, to make loving mankind any easier, to show men as worth dying in agony for. Whatever the initial shrinking was, he got it under control: from now till he died on the Cross, he is master of himself and so of the situation, though his suffering grew worse to the point of desolation.

Peter, ordered to put up his sword, was the first to feel that change—the severed ear, all that remained of his promise to die for his Master, was restored. It was the last healing miracle that we see Christ perform.

To Judas, the betrayer, he said, "Friend, why are you here?"—the only time we hear him address anyone as friend. Is that mere chance? Was it, perhaps, one last effort to save Judas's soul? Was it one element in making him see the evil of the thing he had done and so bringing him to suicide? Not that they would not have killed his Master anyhow. All Judas had done was save them a little trouble.

All the accounts of the preliminary examinations—in the house of Annas and before the Sanhedrin—should be read again and again. So compressed is the telling that there is not one of them in which we do not every so often come upon something we had overlooked.

2.

And there is no end to what one keeps seeing new in the accounts of Calvary itself. I have told the story in *The Church and I* of a street-corner meeting in Walham Green, one of London's less spectacular suburbs. A member of the crowd said: "On the Cross, Christ was unnecessarily melodramatic: he made too much fuss." I doubt if in nineteen centuries anyone else has ever made that comment. As I remember, the speaker on the platform was so startled that all he could think to say was, "If ever you come to be crucified, I hope you will set us all an example of quiet good taste."

The questioner would indeed have found it hard to match the example Christ himself set. He is so incredibly, so fascinatingly, correct! At the first blow on the face, he raises a point of order: "Why strike me unless I have done something wrong? If I have, show me." That is the last comment we hear from him on the savagery of his treatment. He complains of nothing, blames no one, judges no one, is wholly judged. All the taunting drew no word or sign from him. He answered only those who were entitled to question him.

When Caiaphas, the high priest, opened the examination: "I adjure you by the living God, tell us if you are the Christ, the Son of God," Jesus not only did not deny it, he made it worse! "But," he went on, "hereafter you will see the Son seated at the right hand of Power, and coming on the clouds of heaven." The high priest tore his robes, crying out, "Why do we still need witnesses? You have now heard his blasphemy." The tearing of the robes was purely symbolic; it meant tearing a few inches from the neck downward, put there for the purpose: but ritually it was shattering.

Read carefully John's account of the trial, if that be the word, before Pilate. The Roman procurator was bothered —bothered, I think, at being so powerfully impressed by the carpenter. Questioned about his claim to be king, Christ answered, since the procurator was within his rights in asking it. But at the question, "Where are you from?" (asked, apparently, because the prosecution had said that the accused claimed to be the Son of God), Christ remained silent. Pilate said, "Do you not know that I have power to release you and power to crucify you?" Jesus answered: "You would have no power over me unless it were given you from on high; therefore he who delivered me to you has the greater sin." Who was that? Caiaphas, probably. They would hardly have bothered to tell Pilate about Judas.

But the implication that Pilate was also guilty, if less so, must have shaken the procurator, spoken so calmly by the prisoner out of the last dregs of his strength—for a Roman scourging usually killed. Yes, Pilate was being judged indeed. So was just about every man involved in the last scenes. It would be a chance lost if we did not take the opportunity to take a careful look at each of them, then at ourselves.

Of what the victim was suffering physically, we hear nothing from him, unless it be his "I thirst"—even in that he may not have been referring to his parched throat, though the soldiers naturally thought he was. "Jesus, knowing that all was now finished, said to fulfill the Scripture, 'I thirst.' "

Astonishingly, none of the Evangelists make any comment on his sufferings either. They merely record them, making no more appeal for sympathy than he did. By the time they had come to write their Gospels, they knew how vast a thing was happening on Calvary. It was the sacrifice of mankind's redemption, affecting every human being that had been born from the world's beginning or would be born till its end. All the appalling details were on the outer circumference, to be recorded but not lingered over.

Did he feel like that about himself? We must be careful about imagining what was going on inside him, we could so easily be simply imagining him reacting as we should if we had been he—that is, if we had been the God-man! But at least we can concentrate on what we hear him say. And for me it seems evident that while the agony was the condition in which it all happened, the central core of his

being must have been concentrated on the mighty work
he was doing, on the Father *to* whom, and the human race
for whom, he was offering himself. The offering was what
he was doing, the rest was being done to him.

3.

It is odd how many of us would find it hard to remember
all seven of the words he uttered in the three hours he
hung on the Cross. We have a general impression of their
splendor, but each can tell us something, not only about
him but as I think, about what he saw himself as doing.

Three of the seven were about others. The first of them
is clearly to do with redemption.

Father forgive them, for they know not what they do
(Luke 23:34). All the men concerned in his slaying were
members of the race he was dying for. To the end of time
sinners can cling to that word, their last shred of hope that
God may see it so.

This day you will be with me in Paradise (Luke 23:42).
Sinners can cling to that too. He was talking to one of the
murderers being crucified with him, one who had joined
the other in reviling him for not using his power, if he had
it, to save all three. He had the most spectacular of all
deathbed repentances, with his "Lord, remember me
when you come into your kingdom."

This second word has to do with redemption too. Has
the third, spoken to his Mother and the disciple he loved?

Woman behold your son,
Behold your mother (John 19:26-27).

We have already seen that this could not have been an afterthought, as if it had suddenly occurred to him that he had completely forgotten to make any provision for his Mother and must interrupt his offering of himself for the whole world's redemption to do something about it. Could he have said it from the Cross, if the Cross had not been the right place to say it? We know already, and shall see more closely, that we are none of us meant to be only spectators at our own redemption, contributing nothing. We all have our contribution to make, Mary more than all.

The sneering and the taunting were going on all the time. He heard them perhaps, but if I may quote from *To Know Christ Jesus,* much as a priest at the moment of Consecration might hear people talking or a baby crying at the back of the church.

The last four words have no reference to the people present on Calvary, no direct reference at least—but everything said and done on the Cross has reference to all of us.

My God, my God, why hast thou forsaken me?

Christians have been gazing at those words ever since. Were they a cry from him as he reached the ultimate desolation in which he felt that his Father had gone from him? Was he uttering the cry of the mankind with whose need he had so totally identified himself?

We must all read it for ourselves: I can but record my own mind on it. The words are the opening words of Psalm 22. My immediate reaction, when at last I learned this, was that a cry extorted in the extremest desolation was unlikely to be a quotation!

To quote the opening words was a normal way of reference to the whole psalm. Which raises two questions: (1) What did the words mean in the psalm? (2) Why did Christ choose that psalm to quote at that moment?

The psalmist is not saying that God has left him: the next words are, "Why art thou so far from helping me?" Why, in other words, is God letting his enemies do all this to him? What *are* they doing to him? The psalm is an even more detailed description of what is now happening to Christ than Isaiah 53: "All those who see me mock at me—he committed his cause to the Lord, let him rescue him—all my bones are out of joint—they have pierced my hands and my feet—they divide my garments among them, and for my raiment they cast lots."

All these things had happened on Calvary. Even *I thirst* is there—"my tongue cleaves to my throat"—was that why he quoted it? None of his enemies would have failed to recognize the details. And the rest of the psalm would have given them no comfort. While its first half is a desperate cry for God's help, its second is all exultation over the cry answered—"He has not despised the affliction of the afflicted; he has not hidden his face from him but has heard, when he cried to him . . . ." and the psalm goes on to all that God will do for his glory.

    It is finished (John 19:30).
    Father, into thy hands I commit my spirit (Luke 23:46).

All the suffering that came from obedience ends in a cry of love of the Father he had been obeying. The Greek word, translated finished, means consummated, completed. The work he had been sent by the Father to do he had faithfully done. There had been a breach between God and the human race. He had effected at-one-ment (which we disguise by pronouncing it "atonement"). In the man Christ Jesus, God and man were at one.

It is possible to give the whole of our attention to the sufferings Christ endured, and give no thought to all that they effected—for himself, and so for us. In our effort to find out what life is all about, it is essential to find out what Calvary is all about.

One way is to unwrap Paul's "Christ has loved us and has delivered himself for us, an oblation (offering) and a sacrifice to God" (Eph. 5:2). This was *the* sacrifice, the ultimate sacrifice to which all the Old Testament sacrifices were tending, containing in itself all that they were striving toward, effecting in reality all and more than all that they were striving to effect in symbol. With Calvary, their function as foreshadowings, the best possible in the circumstances, was ended. It seems to be a mere chance of history that the Temple sacrifices did cease to be offered by the Jews so soon after Christ's death, with the Roman destruction of the Temple.

Christ's sacrifice contains the Old Testament idea of sacrifice and goes beyond, just as the Trinity contains God as far as the Old Testament shows him and goes beyond. Christ "made all things new" (Rev. 21:5)—including our knowledge of God, including sacrifice.

But in being made perfect the essence of sacrifice was not destroyed. It lives on in its perfecting. The word

means "making sacred"—transferring the object sac-
rificed to the ownership of God, as a way of symbolizing
God's dominion over all things. In our common-sense way
we may wonder what point there could be in offering him
what was already his. Yet it was a genuine sacrifice in our
modern, highly unreligious use of the word, which means
giving up (reluctantly or heroically, as it may happen)
something we value. In the sacrifices alike of pagan and
Jew, men gave up something of value—bull or sheep or
whatever it might be—something they could have used as
their own; they denied themselves that use, in order to
give honor to God.

How could they know that God accepted their sacrifice? Twice indeed in the Old Testament (Lev. 9:24 and
2 Chron. 7:1) we read of God's showing acceptance—by
sending down fire from heaven to the ecstatic joy of
priests and people. Usually it was taken for granted: if the
ritual prescriptions—the animal without blemish, the
words, the actions—had been fulfilled, God's acceptance
could be assumed.

Yet at Scripture's opening came Cain's sacrifice which
was not accepted by God, Abel's which was. And the
prophets had continued the warning: external correctness
was not enough. Isaiah (1:11) records God as saying, "I do
not delight in the blood of bulls . . . I cannot endure [the
combination of] iniquity and solemn assembly . . . cease
to do evil, learn to do good, seek justice, correct oppres-
sion, defend the fatherless, plead for the widow."

Hosea (6:61) records the same warning. "I desire stead-
fast love and not sacrifice, the knowledge of God rather
than burnt offerings." Neither Isaiah nor Hosea means

that God does not want sacrifice but only a clean heart: they are using a Hebrew way of saying that sacrifices without a clean heart are hateful to God. Christ's quoting of Hosea (Matt. 9:13, 12:7) we may take as a warning to ourselves in our attendance at Mass.

Two further points we may notice. The first is that the slaying of the victim (the immolation) need not be done by the priest: it could be done by others, the Temple servants, for instance: but the offering (the oblation) could be made only by the priest.

Second: What was to be done with the victim after it had been offered to God? What use could God make of a blood-drained sheep or a roasted bull? There were various regulations for disposal: but it was hard to preserve the full symbolism of giving to God.

5.

Christ gave himself to death for a sinful world. We have the Baptist saying, "Behold the Lamb of God, who takes away the sin of the world." In the Mass "sin" is changed to "sins," but there really was a sin of the world, an essence of sin all but universal in mankind, lying between, damaging the relations between, the race and God.

Genesis shows the flood of sin that poured out of Adam's disobedience. Even those who do not accept Genesis can see the truth of its picture of a race not one with God—some of its members closer to him than others, some wholly turned from him, but all with a defect in the will, which may be either yielded to or constantly struggled against; it is a will to self, a self-love, which corrodes at once obedience, love of God, love of other people. All of us have to cope with it, somehow.

On the Cross, Christ offering himself for the whole people in the sinfulness that lay between them and God, confronted all three corrosions: he was obedient unto death; his last word was of love of God—"Father, into thy hands I commit my spirit"; three times his concern is for other people—his sinless Mother, the repentant thief, his unrepentant torturers.

This obedience-love syndrome he had acclaimed in a kind of lyrical rapture, in the last half of John's fourteenth chapter: "If you love me, you will keep my commandments." "If a man loves me, he will keep my word and my Father will love him and we will come to him and make our home with him." He feels it as a flowing of life from his Father to himself and to each of us—"I in my Father and you in me and I in you."

The rapture is glorious. But so is his emergence from it into plain statement of linked obedience and love as the meaning of all that is to follow: "I do as the Father has commanded me, so that the world may know that I love the Father. Let us go hence"—to the testing in Gethsemane, to the death on Calvary.

So Christ as Priest offered himself as Victim, slain by others, to his heavenly Father for our sins. No priests in the Old Testament could match this Priest, no victim this Victim. Nor could any acceptance by God match this one. God showed his pleasure in this Victim not by sending fire from heaven but by raising him to life. Death had taken the Victim but God would not let it hold him; the grave had received him, but the grave had to yield him up.

Forty days later, Christ ascended to his Father. This was a constitutive element in the offering's perfection, yet the foreshadowings could contain not so much as a hint of it. As we have noted, God could show his pleasure in the fact of offering: but what could he do with the victims? Only now could he take to himself the Victim offered. There was no question, as in the Temple sacrifices, of how to dispose of the remains. The body slain on Calvary, and the soul separated for a brief while by death, are at the right hand of the Father—which is a way of saying that they are closer to God than any creature ever had been or could be. For they are where the Person is whose soul and body they are.

The Resurrection was not simply a happy postscript to a tragic story; the Ascension not simply a spectacular way of showing that Christ had left our earth in triumph. Each was as necessary to the work to be accomplished as the sufferings unto death which preceded them. What did they accomplish?

Remember the obedience-love linkage hymned by Christ at the Last Supper (John 14: second half). Now read chapter 5 of the Epistle to the Hebrews: *Though he was Son, he learnt obedience by the things he suffered; and being made perfect he became the source of eternal salvation to all who obey him.*

How could the most extreme piety leave us comatose under the two shocks of this? There was obedience he had not yet learned before his passion and death, there was perfection he had not yet attained.

We have heard him say, "I have come to do the will of my Father"; obedience was so evidently both the rule of his life and its joy. What had he to learn about obedience? What could he conceivably have had to learn? He never tells us. But the Epistle was not given to us in order to be ignored. I think we can catch a glimpse of one possible meaning. There is something to be learned about obedience by suffering for it and dying for it. There may be no way of putting into words what has been learned. But obedience would have a new dimension, not statable in terms of the physics of our common spirituality. It would be a new thing. As would the man who had experienced it.

That is what the Epistle says happened to Christ: he was made perfect, he was himself the first beneficiary of his own suffering and death. We must walk delicately here. We cannot know the inner life of a God-man. But for my own encouragement I repeat, this was not shown to us that we might get nothing from it.

Simply looking close at what is there, we begin to wonder if this lay behind his insistence that he must die. In that lay, as we have always realized, the way to salvation for mankind. But we had not perhaps realized that it was the way to his own perfection; and that it was only *as* perfect that he could win our salvation.

Did he realize this when we first meet him in the public life? Perfection meant a total union of his human will with God's divine will, a union whose flowering is love, a flowering not to be attained without obedience. Obedience and love he taught his listeners steadily. Was he talking to himself as well as to them? In the Sermon on the Mount he had told his hearers that they must be perfect as their heavenly Father is: was he thinking of the perfection he too had still to attain?

In a book I wrote on the Lord's Prayer, I raised the question whether it was only a prayer he had given us to pray or had he prayed it himself? Did he ever say to his Father, "Forgive me my trespasses as I forgive. . ."? The question may shock us. He could say in full assurance, "Who can convict me of sin?" But, actual sin apart, did he sometimes feel that he might have done his Father's will more perfectly, even more willingly? Did he ever long to love his Father more? What lover is ever satisfied with the quality of his loving?

Let me repeat, if only for my own satisfaction, the words of Hebrews: "Though he was Son, he learnt obedience by the things he suffered; and being made perfect he became the source of eternal salvation to all who obey him."

This links with what Paul told the Romans about the Resurrection at the beginning of his letter. God's Son "was constituted Son of God in power according to the Spirit of holiness by his resurrection from the dead." From the first moment of his existence in Mary's womb, he was Son of God. What does Son of God *in power* mean? I think it flows out of the perfection that is now his—he is at last established in the existence as man which was proper to the only-begotten Son of God. Fulfilled in himself, he can become the source of salvation to all who join their wills with his in the obedience whose flowering is love.

But just how do we come in? That his sufferings brought him to perfection we can understand. But how can his sufferings make us any different?

CHAPTER SEVEN

Rebirth

1.

In the man Christ Jesus—made perfect by his sufferings, made Son of God in power by his Resurrection—atonement is complete, God and man wholly at one.

In the man Christ Jesus.

But how do we come in? He had "laid down his life for his sheep"—us. "He was to be a source of salvation to all who obey him"—us, we hope. We have noted that we cannot know what life is about till we know what Calvary is about. But what's the connection?

His obedience, his love, his courage were wonderful, but they were his, not ours. Is there some sort of heavenly bookkeeping by which his earnings were to be written into our account? It would be pleasant, of course. But it would be a fiction.

The answer is surprising. We have to be born again. Read how Christ told this to Nicodemus (John 3:1-10). "Unless we are born again we *cannot* enter the Kingdom of God." The idea was totally new, as new as anything Christ ever said. The Old Testament knows nothing of it. The learned Pharisee had never heard of it, to him rebirth could mean only getting back into the womb and coming out again.

87

Observe Christ's word "again," observe the "cannot"—especially the word "cannot." By birth we are members of the human race. And that is not enough. Sin has made such a mess of the race that its members cannot reach the goal for which it exists, *unless* they experience another birth: they must be reborn as members of Christ.

"Water and the Holy Spirit" is the way of it: for forty years or more before John wrote of Christ's telling this to Nicodemus (sixty if he really did write his Gospel as late as the nineties), the Church had been baptizing—as Christ's final instructions had commanded. "Going teach all nations, baptizing them. . . ." Nineteen hundred years later it still is. And so till the last human child is born. Even before Matthew wrote those instructions at the end of his Gospel, Paul had told the Galatians (3:27), "In Christ Jesus you are all sons of God through faith. For as many of you as were baptized into Christ *have put on Christ.*"

It was a daring phrase: we are in Christ Jesus, not as our body is in our clothes but as our cells are in our body. That is what the word Christ-ening, which we disfigure with the pronunciation chrissening, says. Christ did not come slumming among us to do whatever he could for us before returning where he belonged: he went down to man's level to bring him up, not simply up to his own level but into his very self. The putting on of Christ was a real renaturing, as Paul went straight on to tell the Galatians—"there is neither Jew nor Greek, there is neither slave nor free, there is neither male nor female"—all these distinctions belong to the nature you were born in; now reborn, "you are all *one* in Christ

Jesus"—the Greek is to be read as meaning one person.

We might pause here—to take breath, of course, if this line of Christ's thinking about us is new to us; but also to weigh what it is saying, to decide whether we feel any inclination to go any deeper into it. This talk of "neither Jew nor Greek" may rub against a pretty strong feeling already instinctive in some; so may "neither male nor female"; so may "neither management nor worker."

Quite apart from that, really devout people may feel that these depths are not for them; they have no muscles for swimming so deep, no lungs: they are in good relations with God and their friends as it is. Why introduce complications? Think hard before making any such decision. These things are the reality of yourselves as Christians— of yourselves, and your wives or husbands and children. We have already seen that it would be strange to love God and have no desire to know him better. It would be strange to love anybody, oneself or others, without desiring at least to know what you, they, really are. For make no mistake, this being "in Christ" *is* the reality of you, me. The New Testament has the phrase round fifty times.

What does it mean? What can it mean? Christ had prepared the Apostles for it with "I am the life": a curious word *am* in this context. Had he said I have the life we could have asked him, Please Lord, give it to us: since he says I *am* the life we can only ask Please, Lord, live in us. He is not to *give* us life as parents give life to their children, he is to live in us: he is not giving us life similar to his, he is giving us his.

And what is his? Not the natural life of the body, not

even the natural life of intellect and will: any of the three would be merely developments of the life that is ours by our birth into the human race. It is the life that was his by the indwelling in his soul of the Holy Spirit: the life in him without which no man can come to the Father (John 14:6). The Holy Spirit living in Christ is to live in us.

In all ages the Holy Spirit had given light and strength to men's souls. Till Christ revealed that he was a distinct person, the Chosen People could think of him only as God at work in them. The word spirit—*pneuma* in Greek, *ruah* in Hebrew—meant breath: they had read in Genesis that God breathed on the man he had formed of dust and he became a living soul: they hardly saw it as a constituent element, the life-giving element, in man or animal: God breathed in a man and he was alive; God withdrew his breath and the man was dead.

Clearly the Apostles did not at once know that the Spirit their Master talked of was more than that, nor did he at first tell them. It was already a vast effort for them to realize that there was a Second Self within the Oneness which it had been Israel's mission to champion in a world of gods beyond number. Till they had given their minds to that, they could have made nothing of a Third. At the Last Supper it may well have been a shock to all of them to hear Christ say, "When he, the Spirit of Truth is come, he will lead you into all truth": the Greek word for spirit we have just noted, is *pneuma*, a neuter noun: they would have expected "it." "He" left no doubt that a distinct Person was in question.

However that may be, by the time his Gospel was

written, John knew of the three Selves within the Oneness, and was writing in a Church which had long been
baptizing in their name. In that knowledge he wrote a
sentence which in the general magnificence may not have
caught our attention. "This he said about the Spirit which
those who believed in him were to receive; for as yet the
Spirit had not been given, because Jesus was not yet
glorified" (7:39).

This clearly was what Christ meant when at the Last
Supper he told the Apostles that if he did not go, the Spirit
would not come. Christ could work miracles in the order
of nature, even bring the dead to life, but the life of the
Spirit he could not give till he was "glorified" at the
Father's right hand, made perfect by his sufferings, made
Son of God in power by his Resurrection. At the first
meeting after his Resurrection, he "breathed on them and
said, 'Receive the Holy Spirit.'" Fifty days later the Holy
Spirit descended on them in the form of tongues of fire.

2.

Strange how the notion of the Kingdom of God has
faded out of the general Christian consciousness. John the
Baptist had been baptizing in Jordan, calling on all to
repent because the Kingdom of God was at hand. Christ
opened his own preaching mission with exactly the same
announcement. In the Lord's Prayer he tells us to ask the
Father, "Thy kingdom come."

It was not for preaching it that his enemies wanted him
dead, but it was the reason they chose as likely to cause
Pilate to have him crucified. In all four Gospels his open-

ing question was, "Are you the king of the Jews?" This runs as a motif all through the trial. The soldiers in mockery put a robe of purple on his shoulders and a crown of thorns on his head. Twice Pilate presented him to the crowd, "Here is your king" and "Shall I crucify your king?" He had "Jesus of Nazareth king of the Jews" affixed to the Cross. Hanging there Jesus heard the taunt, "Christ, king of Israel, come down from the Cross." And the repentant bandit said, "Remember me when you come into your kingdom." The last words the Apostles said before his Ascension were, "Will you at this time restore the kingdom to Israel?"

A series of changes or chances has caused the word kingdom to be no longer a vital element in the life of most Christians. It has passed from the mind's forefront to the shadowy places of memory. When Christ first used it, his Jewish hearers could only think joyfully of the restoration of David's kingdom: to Gentiles also, from the dawn of recorded history, while kingship meant a special relation with the gods, kingdoms were very much of this world. But in our world, even where the title of king is still to be found—it conveys no very obvious relation to the kingdom Christ talked of. For Christians that means the Church, whether the visible church of Catholics and Eastern Orthodox, or the invisible church of all who accept Christ as their Saviour. But this lay in the future. "Kingdom of God" is all over the Gospels: sometimes it is called "Kingdom of Heaven," used because their awareness of God's majesty made Jews unwilling to utter the word God, as Catholics have a fear of cheapening the name Jesus by overuse.

Observe that, like so much else in the Gospels, it is new. It is not in the Old Testament. Kingdom indeed is there, but a kingdom very definitely of this world. Christ could say to Pilate, "My kingdom is not of this world"; David could not have said that. So what did Christ mean by it?

It is not an oversimplification to say that in the Lord's Prayer "Thy kingdom come" is one way of saying what the petition immediately after it says more clearly, "Thy will be done." Wherever God's will is obeyed, there God reigns, his authority acknowledged. That is the kingdom. That is what we pray may become reality over all the world *as it is in heaven.* The union of men's will with God's is the point: the union of men, thus obedient to God, with one another *is* the kingdom.

For citizenship there must be repentance—the Greek word is *metanoia,* a change in the *nous,* a change of mind and heart, the heart centered upon God as Christ's was and no longer on self: but it is not to be an invisible kingdom living only in the hearts of men. It is indeed not of this world, its root is in God himself, but it is very definitely *in* this world: Christ spoke of his kingdom as having a structure here upon earth. He spoke to Nicodemus of entry by rebirth of water and the Holy Spirit, of publicans and harlots admitted before scribes and Pharisees. In granting the headship of the kingdom on earth to Peter, he gives him the keys of "the Kingdom of Heaven."

And in general we find that phrase used of what we may think of as the kingdom's novitiate, or first stage, the Church on earth. Failure to grasp this causes the odd

notion—flowering in so many jokes, not all very funny—
that Peter has the keys of heaven itself, so that when we
die we shall find him at heaven's gate, either admitting us
or directing us elsewhere.

In what Christ says of the kingdom he moves easily
from the kingdom already existent in heaven to the one he
is in process of founding on earth. When the Pharisees
asked him when the kingdom was coming, he said, "The
Kingdom of God is not coming with signs to be observed
. . . behold, the Kingdom of God is in the midst of you"
(Luke 17:20). So it was there already, for in essence the
kingdom is himself, and it is by being reborn into him that
we enter it.

At the Last Supper we hear him say to the Apostles, "As
my Father has appointed me a kingdom, so do I appoint
for you that you may eat and drink at my table in my
Kingdom" (Luke 22:29).

And at the judgment he will say to those who have fed
the hungry, "Come, O blessed of my Father, inherit the
Kingdom prepared for you from the foundation of the
world" (Matt. 25:34).

The kingdom has its structure, and its officials. But
neither structure nor officials are its meaning. The officials are to serve: the structure exists for the sake of the
life, which he had come that we might have. "He has
delivered us from the dominion of darkness and trans-
ferred us to the Kingdom of his Son's love, in whom we
have redemption, the forgiveness of sins" (Col. 1:3). Redemption, forgiveness, those are what the kingdom is
about. Officials caught up in the immensely complicated

business of keeping the kingdom running have been known to forget this.

3.

Just as we should be wrong to see redemption as saving us by the barrel load, we should be wrong to see it as wholly individual, simply ourself and God. We are all in-lived by the same Christ, all drawing the same life from the same source: by that shared membership of Christ we are linked to one another. Christ uses the figure of a grapevine, Paul of a human body, the point being the same in both: all elements in vine or body live by the one life: with development in biology we have come to think of the members of Christ as cells in a body, all made alive by *his* life.

To repeat: we are not members of his physical body, the one conceived in the virgin's womb, dead on the Cross, now at the right hand of the Father, received by us in Communion. His Church is a social body, each cell a person, but all living by the life of the One *whose body it is*.

If the idea is new to us it is worth lingering on. It is mysterious all right: we call the Church the *Mystical* Body of Christ. St. Augustine has reminded us that by it we are more closely related to Christ than even his Mother was merely by the physical relation of conceiving: "More blessed was Mary in receiving Christ into her heart than by conceiving him in her body." And we are more closely related to one another in Christ, I to you, you to me, than by natural relation.

Think further. This second life does not annihilate the
first and take its place—how much simpler for us if it did!
It enters into the first to give us new powers. We do not
cease to be the same man we were and become another
man.

We have the same intellect by which we know, but with
the new power of *faith,* the power to accept what God
reveals simply because it is his.

We have the same will by which we love, but with the
new power which Paul calls *charity,* by which we love
God for being God, love him with a love which can spread
to embrace all men, a beginning in us of the love Christ
has for them.

And operating at once out of intellect and will, we have
the new power of *hope*—knowing that Christ wants to
save us, wanting him to.

These three virtues are hymned for us in the thirteenth
chapter of 1 Corinthians. They relate us directly to God
and flow into our relations with one another.

Prudence, justice, temperance, fortitude, these virtues
bear directly on our contacts with others and with the
whole of creation. *Prudence* is not what it has been
weakened down to—playing safe, avoiding having to use
the virtue of fortitude: it means seeing situations aright:
guided by it we might see that the prudent course in a
given situation would be to be a martyr. *Justice* is fairness
in all our dealings. *Temperance* is self-control, preventing
us from letting our desires enslave us, drink, sex, money,
praise. *Fortitude* is self-control, too, facing not evading
whatever pain of soul or body obedience to God's will may
cause us.

These seven are all virtues and supernatural. They have
their grounds in our nature, rightly called by the same
names but without either the light or the strength or the
outflowing from God's love. All are virtues—the word
comes from the Latin *vir*, man: we are more fully human
for having them.

The life into which we are reborn has not only the
powers at which we have been glancing. It has needs, too,
statable in the same terms as for the first life—for tending,
nourishment, exercise. For the moment we concentrate
on the sacraments.

4.

These are used by Christ because of the double
nature—material, spiritual—that he and we both have.
He will not let us forget, as he did not, that we have
bodies. That they are there, we are of course in no danger
of forgetting; they won't let us. But we may easily forget
that they have their part not only in our created pleasures
and pains, but in our approach to God in worship.

It is not the soul that approaches God but the self. It is
not the soul to which God responds but the self. In our
approach and in his response the body is an essential
element in the self. One has heard Baptism, the Christ-
ening by which we become members of Christ, mocked as
wetting a baby's head. There is nothing merely comic
about a head, nothing merely comic about water. Both are
essential to the natural life of mankind. That God, the
author of both, should bring them together at a decisive

point in human life, the point of rebirth, seems comic only to one who has never seen below the surface of anything.

It is simple sense that God, having made us a union of matter and spirit, should approach us spiritually in material things and actions. That the Holy Spirit should come to us in the pouring of water gives a new sacredness to water, a reminder that our body too is sacred. We have no need to be told of the evil that comes from concentrating on the body and neglecting the mind. The contrary evil, which comes from despising the body, seeing it *as* an evil, seeing all hope in liberation from it, may not be so obvious to us. It is in the balance—seeing spirit as primary, but the body too as sacred—that health lies: as the sacraments are a continuing reminder.

Observe how closely they follow the shape, the curvature, so to say, of our natural life. Baptism "matches" our birth, Confirmation our maturing, Orders and Matrimony the choice of a way of life, Anointing, sickness and death. In among them comes Penance for healing, Eucharist for daily food.

Baptism and Eucharist are the two that Christ introduces with the warning word "unless"—"Unless one be born again of water and the Holy Spirit, he cannot enter into the Kingdom of God" (John 3:5). "Unless you eat the flesh of the Son of man and drink his blood, you shall not have life in you. He who eats my flesh and drinks my blood has eternal life, and I will raise him up at the last day for my flesh is meat indeed, and my blood is drink indeed" (John 6).

Warnings of that solemnity—"cannot enter the Kingdom of Heaven," "shall not have life in you"—cannot be brushed aside as though they had never been spoken.

Meditating on them the Church has seen a mitigation of their starkness. As we read them we might think that one who through no fault cannot receive Baptism or Eucharist—namely, the vast majority of the human race—was doomed to eternal loss with never a chance of salvation. The millions on millions of adults who have never heard of either, infants dying unbaptized—these are obvious cases. It would be strange for the Saviour of mankind to impose a condition for salvation which the overwhelming majority literally could not meet.

And short of literally—there is the smaller but still considerable number of those who have heard of both, but in a context—of history or upbringing—in which their acceptance would be close to a moral impossibility, in which some even feel it their duty to Christ to deny both.

The Church, meditating on this message, saw that the absoluteness of Christ's statements was an example of a teaching method which was normal in the Jewish world—the use of exaggeration for emphasis, to make sure that the point was taken. Modifications, qualifications, adaptations to the vast complexities of the human condition, could follow: each human being *is* a different problem, to be judged differently: the divine Physician gives rules of health for all, but he treats each case as he finds it. "Come to me, all you who labor and are heavy laden, and I will give you rest."

St. Augustine sums it up: "We are bound by the sacraments, God is not." If they are out of our reach, God has other ways.

But it still remains clear that Christ thought them the

best way. Let us look closely to see why he thought them so. We owe this to ourselves; we owe it to all for whom we could shed light on them: it would be a pity if we, either by refusal to help or by explaining badly, were part of the context which accounts for their refusing either gift.

Baptism we have been considering. Let us consider the Eucharist. We have just heard its "unless," spoken just after the feeding of the five thousand. At the Last Supper Christ told *how* they might eat his flesh and drink his blood. Only John does not include this in his account of the Supper—perhaps because he had already given the "unless" in his chapter 6.

The other three and Paul (1 Cor. 11:23,25) have Christ using somewhat different words of consecration: my own guess is that he said them all and varying selections were made: in any event, each Gospel, like Paul's Epistle, makes clear that the consecrated bread *is* his body, the consecrated wine *is* his blood, poured out for the forgiveness of sins; and that the Apostles also are to consecrate and give Christ thus really present to be received by worshipers.

Christians came to speak of the Real Presence, using the word real as opposed to symbolic. There have been those who have given explanations of "presence" to explain that the body and blood are not actually there. But note that the Gospels do not use the term Real Presence at all: they have Christ saying, "my body," "my blood." Paul has the same words with the comment, "Whoever eats the bread or drinks the cup of the Lord in an unworthy manner will be guilty of profaning the body and blood of the Lord . . . . Anyone who eats and drinks without discerning the body, eats and drinks judgment upon himself" (1 Cor. 11:27-29).

One other point before we come to why eternal life is involved in the reception of the Eucharist: "eat the flesh" and "drink the blood," says Our Lord. Through the centuries the Church has normally given the sacrament to the congregation under the form of bread only: the reason being that Christ now lives eternally, so that where his body is there he wholly is—blood and soul and divinity. We cannot receive either the body or the blood without receiving the other: in the early Church infants, dying, received the sacrament in the form of a drop of wine on the tongue. To insist that receiving the blood into ourself in union with the body is not the same as drinking seemed to her an overemphasis on the act of drinking, whereas the reception of the blood into ourselves is what matters. However that may be, reception under both forms is increasingly common.

But why is it all so important? We may feel that to receive Christ thus totally within ourselves is so splendid that it needs no analyzing. If we do analyze, each one of us may do it differently. The line that appeals to me begins from the truth that each life has, and can only be nourished by, the food appropriate to it. We feed our body with bodily food—with proteins and such, not with ideas. We feed our minds with ideas, not with proteins. But what food could nourish a life which *is* Christ? Only Christ himself surely, which the Eucharist is.

For our own personal nourishment, sanctification, salvation, the value of the Eucharist is clear. Paul gives us a larger reason—"Because there is one bread, we who are many are one body, for we all partake of the one bread" (1 Cor. 10:17). It is the food not only of each of us, but of the church—the "one person" which we are in Christ.

CHAPTER EIGHT

Coredeemers

So far we have been concentrating on what membership of the Body offers its members, in what cellship offers the cells—us. To a person with no unduly clamorous bodily appetites to distract him, the life of liturgy and sacrament and doctrine could be a very luxurious life indeed.

But a body does not exist for the sake of its cells. They are there for the sake of the body; and both cells and body exist for the sake of the person—you, me—in this wholly special instance, Christ.

1.

Why did Christ choose to have this second Body? Clearly there was work still needing to be done in the world, and he saw this as the way to do it. In his life here he worked through the body he got from his Mother: taught in it, suffered in it, died to redeem mankind in it. All this—the teaching, the suffering, the redeeming has to go on. He does it till time shall end, through the Body; his Mystical Body is the successor and continuator of his natural body.

The natural body failed him often enough—through no fault of its own: circumstances pressed it beyond a body's capacity to respond. Nor has his Mystical Body done his work in the world with any very resounding success. Two thousand years after, says the recent Vatican Council, there are two thousand million people in the world who have never heard of him: and, of the minority who have heard of him, vast numbers are not drawn to him, and other vast numbers seem to be moving away if not from Christ, certainly from his Body.

We are warned that we must not judge by figures. Whether the warning is sound or not, the figures can only depress. Certainly, what is happening in the depths of souls and in the depths of societies is what matters, and it is beyond our gaze—which does not entitle us to assume that if it were visible it would turn the dreary picture into a success story. For practical purposes it is better to assume that the cells of the Body—we and the rest—have failed. Through no fault of our own?

Let us consider.

"Going, make disciples of all nations, teaching them . . . ." He wanted the truth spread, the truth to which he had come (remember?) to bear witness, the truth which is to make men free. "Going," Christ said. He did not say, "Have the truth ready to distribute to any who come for it": "Go" is his word: "go and find them, bring my teaching to them, offer them rebirth in me." It would be too much to say that only in the underdeveloped countries is there any large-scale "going," to bring his truths to those who lack them.

Or would it? Anyhow, whether or not the Church has, or the Churches have, at the moment any serious plan for teaching our own nation to observe all things whatsoever

Christ has commanded, what of our individual selves? Have we any urge to bring the gifts—doctrine and moral law and sacraments, Christ himself—even to the people we love?

You may have wondered that I list suffering and redeeming as work Christ continues to do in his Body, the Church, till the end of time. The redemptive sacrifice he offered by his own suffering and death was complete: only he could do it, and he wholly did it: there is nothing to be added to it: in him God and man were at one. But that what he won for the race should be taken and made his own by each individual member of the race, that is an enormous work, never ended. New members are constantly being born into the race; each must be told of Christ's saving work and make his own response to it. Those who have learned and accepted may lose faith or courage: they need continual aid from truth and sacrament.

And we are not meant to be only conveyers of Christ's gifts; they must be living in us if we are to pass them on living. Read and reread Col. 1:24. Every word is saying something vital to you and me, "I rejoice in my sufferings *for your sake.* And in my flesh I complete *what is lacking in Christ's afflictions* for the sake of his body, which is the Church." Two shocks in ten words. Something lacking in Christ's sufferings! Paul proposing to supply it! Coma would have to be very pious indeed not to be shocked into full consciousness.

There was nothing the God-man *could* do that Christ did not do. But he was acting *for* the whole human race, not instead of, not as a substitute. "He bore our sins in his own body on the cross" (1 Peter 2:29)—in taking our sins with him, at a depth we cannot see, he took us with him. We are not meant to be spectators at our race's redemption, the victor gracefully and graciously including us in his victory. What was lacking in Christ's afflictions? Whatever the human race *could and should* suffer with him. Paul would offer his mighty contribution: our own lesser contributions we all have the opportunity to make.

In other words, Paul has restated the problem of pain—not how to avoid it but, given that all will have their share of it, how not to waste it, how to make use of it. If we are willing to offer it to Christ for linking with his own suffering, it can be salvation-bringing.

2.

There is one great way available for all the Church's members if they will to take part in Christ's continuing work of redemption. We took a first look at it in chapter one, observing the oddness of our getting all worked up over changes in the offering of the mass, and not bringing Christ into the argument at all.

On the Cross he said, "It is finished" or "accomplished." But Hebrews tells us (9:12) that he entered heaven *on our behalf*—that is, to do something for us. What was it? Paul tells the Romans (8:34) that he is at the right hand of the Father, "interceding for us," pleading with God for us. Hebrews (7:24) clarifies that—"he holds his priesthood permanently," because he continues forever. *Consequently* he is able "for all time to save those who draw near to God through him" since "he always lives to make intercession for us." "His priesthood continues"—offering the victim was the priestly work, the slaying might be done by others. And in heaven, the offering is continuous—there is no new slaying. He offers himself, once slain on Calvary, now forever living, to his Father, that each member of the race should receive what on Calvary he won for the whole race.

This continuing priesthood of Christ breaks through to our altars at every Mass—the priest, by Christ's command and in his name, offers the same Christ, eucharistically present, to the same heavenly Father for the same purpose. It is beyond compare the most important work Christ does through his Church: and it is our privilege to join the priest and so join Christ himself in the offering he is making in heaven.

Our offering is completed at the consecration and the prayers which follow. With that we can relax and prepare to join with our fellow members of Christ in receiving back for our nourishment the Victim we offered to the Father for our sins.

Every Mass, whatever the details of the ritual, is what I have just described. Ritual details matter, of course, but not in comparison with what Christ and the priest and we are joining in doing. By all means campaign for a better ritual. But not during Mass. While we are offering that, it would be mere frivolity to be thinking of anything else.

Once we have grasped what the Mass is, there is an exhilaration in thinking about it; the question whether or not it should be of obligation no longer arises for us.

Mass is a high point of our service of him. What of all the rest of the things he uses the Body for? The teaching, with which we might bring people close to him, the sacrificing-till-it-hurts for the needy. . . .

It used to be urged against Catholics that the Church called Our Lady "coredemptrix." We were reminded that Paul said, "There is one mediator between God and man, the man Christ Jesus" (1 Tim. 2:5). But those words were preceded by "for," i.e., "because." What did Paul say must happen *because* Christ is the one mediator? "Supplication, prayers, intercessions, and thanksgivings be made for all men." These would avail precisely because of, and in union with, Christ's having given himself as a ransom for all. In other words, Christ wants all of us doing our part with him in the redeeming activity that must go on. We are all called to be coredeemers. To give that title, as the Church occasionally has, to his Mother, is not to make her level with him, but to see her as the holiest of all those he has redeemed.

CHAPTER NINE

The Biology of the New Life

1.

The life in Christ has its own biology which we should try to master. We have been looking at its beginning in us, its powers, its nourishing. Pause upon that last word. This new life, like the one we begin with, can grow in us. For the health of both there are rules, primarily physical for the first, primarily spiritual and moral for the second. Our vitality requires our one self to live the born life and the reborn life together. The physical, spiritual, and moral are interwoven, in a plan of action very complex to analyze, but not complicated in its working—unless we complicate it ourselves. Which of course you and I are doing all the time. We shall talk about that in the next chapter.

The basic rule Christ gives for our lives is the combination of obedience and love which we have seen was the basic rule of his own life and death. Our obedience is the seed, planted in us by grace; love is the fruit of our union with infinite truth and infinite goodness. There is no servility in the obedience, first, because God is infinite reality and to be in tune with reality is the essence of freedom; second, because God does not force us to obey, we can disobey if we choose: the results of disobedience will be harmful *because we have broken away from real-*

ity: there is no health in the unreal.

To his chosen people God had given the Ten Commandments, seven of them put negatively—"you shall not." But he had also given them two which are wholly positive: "You shall love the Lord your God with all your heart and all your soul and all your strength (Deut. 6:4); "You shall love your neighbor as yourself" (Lev. 19:18).

These two Christ took and made the living principle in the ten—"On these depend the Law and the Prophets." Remember how he had stunned his hearers on the Mount by saying, "I have not come to destroy the Law and the Prophets, but to fulfill them"—the most startling words ever to come out of the mouth of an Israelite. This making love to be their life principle was the fulfilment he had promised. So "love is the fulfilling of the law," as Paul told the Romans, those masters of law (13:10): he was saying that the law which does not serve love is a bad law.

Interestingly, Christ never defines love, only tells us the things that flow from it—love above all is to be judged by its fruits. Think of such of these fruits as we have already seen—doing the will of God as instance of the obedience, laying down life for a friend as instance of the love. There are those who do precisely think that the two commands of love make the other Commandments unnecessary. Elsewhere I have told of the man who walked out on wife and family, set up house with a nun: both were daily communicants, convinced that love was the supreme law and that they were fulfilling it.

That, I imagine, may have been in the mind of the official of a large Catholic organization who instructed the members to talk of morality without mentioning sin or

Commandments—the only sin Christ found objectiona-
ble being legalism. But in the best-known instance of his
compassion—I mean the episode of the woman taken in
adultery (John 8:3)—his last words to her were, "Sin no
more." We know what the sin was—a breach of the sixth
commandment. He was not warning her to be less legalis-
tic in future.

The individual commandments in fact—the ten and
such others as he himself gives—are only warnings of
ways in which we fail in love of God or neighbor. A total
failure in either means that our life has failed, with final
loss resultant.

But, interestingly again, nearly all the examples Christ
shows of actions leading to everlasting loss are of failures
in love of neighbor—heartlessness over the hungry, the
thirsty, the naked, the sick, prisoners; hatred and contempt for a brother (Matt. 5:22); not forgiving the wrongs
others have done us. Most of the sins with which Christ
charges scribes and Pharisees in Matthew's chapter 23 are
failures in love of neighbor leading to one of the grimmest
of rhetorical questions, "How are you to escape being
sentenced to hell?"

That is why his answer to "What must I do to have
eternal life?" is "Keep the commandments." When the
rich young man said, "Which?" the answer was the seven
which treat of our neighbor, with the noncoveting of his
wife and goods lumped together (the only time, I think)
into the one command to love your neighbor as yourself
(Matt. 19:17). Similarly, in listing sins which defile, i.e.,
make us dirty, he reels off five of the ten—theft, murder,
adultery, coveting, slander—and adds varieties of

these—evil thoughts, fornication, malice, deceits, lust, envy, pride, and foolishness (Mark 7:21).

Foolishness may strike us as a weak ending to so strong a list. We might link it in our minds with the psalmist's fool "who said in his mind, there is no God" (Psalms 14 and 53); or with the fool of Christ's parable who laid up treasure for himself and forgot about God (Luke 12:20).

In chapter two we noticed the coma, nonpious this one, which shelters us from hearing what we would rather not hear. The instances there given concerned Christ's teaching on riches, the duty of forgiveness, heartlessness about the needs of others, the duty of letting the ninety-nine sheep look after themselves for a bit while the shepherd goes in search of the lost one. I give now one other of the same sort—the misuse of sex—which many a good Christian simply cannot believe that Christ could be wholly serious about.

In one of Nancy Mitford's novels there is a snippet of conversation between a Protestant girl and the quite pious French Catholic with whom she is having an affair. She wonders how the affair can fit with his Catholic faith. "A small sin of the flesh," he says airily. "She was not sure if she liked being just a small sin of the flesh."

All evidence seems to show that this attitude to both adultery and fornication (which is bodily union with no intention of permanence) is being taken increasingly for granted by believers. Christ gives no hint of thinking it a small sin of the flesh. He does not say that sex sins are the worst of sins, but we have just heard him list both among things that defile (befoul, says the Oxford Dictionary). In the Sermon on the Mount, having stated that the man who looks at a woman lustfully has already "committed adultery with her in his heart," he proceeds, "If your eye causes you to sin, pluck it out: it is better than you lose one of your members than that your whole body be cast into hell." He is not, I think, urging self-mutilation: it is an example of that exaggeration for the sake of emphasis which was a norm of Jewish speech: but there is no doubt what truth he was emphasizing.

I repeat: Our Lord does not think the misuse of sex the worst of sins. But he could no more fail than we can to see how few escape its power to attract—the allure of virtue is so very resistible in comparison; nor could he overlook its power to monopolize the mind and the appetite. That, perhaps, would be enough reason for him to call it defiling. But I think there may have been another reason in his mind. Even in marriage, where sex fundamentally belongs, the bodily union *can* be almost wholly selfish—with one partner in the grip of sheer physical craving, the other hardly seen save as a release for that craving. Robert Burns, writing out of an experience of sex wider than most men have had, can write in *Letters to a Young Man:*

> *It hardens all within*
> *And petrifies the feeling.*

To reduce another image of God to the condition of a mere object of one's own physical relief—that precisely is defilement, for both.

2.

We have seen that Christ nowhere gives any definition of love. He speaks mainly in terms of what love does and what the unloving refuse to do. Paul, who seems never to have seen him in his earthly life, had made a microscopic study of every word of Jesus that anyone could report to him. He gives a rich list of qualities beginning with Love *is*—patient and kind, not jealous or boastful, not arrogant or rude, not irritable or resentful. At the end of the list comes a gem—"Love bears all things, believes all things, endures all things." All these are from the thirteenth chapter of 1 Corinthians, about which my excitement cannot have escaped any reader.

Neither Christ nor Paul says anything directly about the emotion, the stir in the feelings, which for most people *is* love. Thinking of love as feeling, they find it difficult to imagine what it means to love God. Feeling about one's friends and enemies is no problem: feeling love for Christ we can make sense of. But love of God, whom we have not seen and of whom we can form no mental picture, seems to give "love" a meaning which it has in relation to no one else. Reverence, awe, gratitude—we have a general notion of what we are saying when we use those words. But love?

The emotional accompaniments, of course, are not love: we only have them because we are a compound of spirit and matter: it is in the border region between them that the emotional excitements flourish (border regions tend to be like that). I have read of an Asiatic people who cannot get interested in English poetry because most of it seems to be about love, and they think of love only as a derangement of the functions of the liver.

Anyhow angels, with no bodies, therefore no border region, cannot have emotions, either the good ones or the bad. We can be stormed by them. But to repeat, they are not the love itself, only its effects in the excitable part of us. Love is in the will. I shall no more try to define it than Christ tried or Paul. I shall not even say why I think it is undefinable. But it *is* recognizable, by two of its effects in us—a desire that the one loved may have what he desires (a union of wills), and a desire to *be with* the other (a union of the selves). And this latter, I think, is the distinctive, decisive element—two realities in living contact.

Should we be depressed if the desire to be with God is not very clamorous in us? Glance back at the discussion in chapter one on whether we feel any very positive desire for Christ's company.

Not much is gained by trying to whip up that particular desire: it should grow out of our lives together, God's and ours. The last five words may sound ridiculous, but they are plain prose. We are never out of God's presence, only his continuing will to hold us in existence prevents our falling back into the nothing which went into our making.

The bare thought of never being out of his sight one may find forbidding:

As ever in my great Task-Master's eye—

sounds more like a slave talking than a son: but Milton was only twenty-three when he wrote it. Sons are what we are, not slaves. We must use our minds to grasp all that we know of God from Christ Our Lord, and live our lives in the light of it. The combination of knowing and living by what we know, testing what we know by living it, will produce its own effect upon the will. I do not know what else can.

Meanwhile, in prayer, we have at our disposal an immediate way of being *with* God. Given that God is never not there, we can start a conversation at any moment. How? If you are accustomed to praying, you will not need to be told. There are the great "set" prayers, prayed by generations—the Lord's Prayer; Acts of Contrition, Faith, Hope, Charity; Psalms, hymns—they may have become routine; they need not remain so. Then there are all the things we want to tell him on our own account: again, we are not likely to find much difficulty in opening ourselves to him. And this is where those can come in who have no present habit of prayer. Just start telling God whatever is on your mind—complain if you will, he has had plenty of that through all the millennia. Start talking. You will feel, often enough, that no one is listening, but you know from your own reasoning, and from Church and Scripture, that God *is* there. Keep talking. Occasionally you *may* get a feeling of absolute certainty that someone is listening—it may be only a feeling, but your knowledge that it is a fact does not depend on feeling.

Conversation cannot consist only of complaints and demands. God helping and you cooperating, real conversation can begin, not simply all that is *on* your mind but anything that is *in* it—about God or other people or yourself. Temperaments vary, but the effort persisted in can grow into a habit and, more slowly, into a need.

Prayer is a way of living with God. And the God we are with is Father and Son and Holy Spirit, living their own eternal life at the very root of our being—the point at which we are no longer nothing but something—causing us to exist, holding us in existence. For Catholics, the high peak of praying is the Mass. And in the Mass almost all the prayers are to the Trinity—*through* Jesus Christ our Lord and Brother.

As we become more alive to Father, Son, and Holy Spirit so that they too become "part of our personal chronicles," praying comes more naturally, adoration and thanksgiving almost automatically. But that can flow only out of bringing our whole mind to bear on all that Scripture and the Church have to teach us: our own experience of living it. It takes us a long while to realize what Christ meant by sending the Holy Spirit as recompense for his own departure. I can offer no rules. We must just work at it. . .

What it all comes to for you and me is the realization that this life in Christ, ourselves indwelt by Father and Son and Holy Spirit as Christ is, is reality: human life, not thus indwelt, could be only a shadow life, without a mainspring, without a goal.

But, to repeat a phrase, reality may call for efforts and resistances in ourselves. We know why Pope Leo the Great could call upon the Christian to realize the greatness that is his. Yet there are times when we wish we could feel like it. Desire says that something with less strain in it would suit our spinelessness better. Judgment says, "Greatness? Us?"

The human will—clutching at what it wants, evading

what it dislikes—has always been the problem for men; also (I say it with reverence) for God. Having given man free will, he *could* not force it.

He made it free, capable of choosing, otherwise of course it would not have been a will! The very phrase free will is a tautology—if not free, then not will. And without that we should not be men. In creating men with wills thus free, and entrusting the universe to them, God took the same risk as Christ took when he entrusted his Church to men. It can only mean that God loves man, Christ loves man. Considering what was to follow—the desertion and denial—it is touching that John introduces the Supper with the words "When Jesus knew that his hour had come to depart out of this world to the Father, having loved his own who were in the world, he loved them to the end."

To understand all the defects in the Church that we so endlessly complain of, we need only study ourselves—for churchmen are men. Our sinfulness caused his death, but his death did not heal it: it made healing possible; but we must do our part. We must face the plain fact as he faced it—we cannot save ourselves without him, but he cannot save us without us.

As it happens, the initial difficulty for us lies in the nature into which we were born. But the life of grace, into which we are reborn in Christ, while it makes eternal salvation possible, certainly begins by complicating things for us here on earth. For it gives us two very different lives to handle.

As we have seen, grace does not abolish our natures as human beings, but inserts a new life principle into them with new powers of action. The trouble is that while grace gives us new powers to act virtuously for the love of God, it does not remove our tendencies to act sinfully for the love of self.

Let us look at ourselves.

CHAPTER TEN

Ourselves in Christ

Rebirth into Christ, which is entry on the Way, is no guarantee that we shall make it to the end. Since I first read it—not so long after he wrote it!—I am haunted by Francis Thompson's

> *There is no expeditious road*
> *To pack and label men for God*
> *And save them by the barrel-load.*

We are born into Christ singly, in Christ we make the choice of salvation singly. Christ died once for all: but the redeeming must go on. With each new human life, it starts all over again. Christ himself earned our salvation, Hebrews reminds us, with tears and groanings and imploring. He didn't use his divinity to sidestep difficulties, neither can we. "*In Christ* we must work out our salvation," says Paul, "with fear and trembling." No "expeditious" road? Francis Thompson hit the center marvelously.

Walking the road of salvation cannot mean lounging into heaven. The efforts and resistances called for may vary from one person to the next; so may the anguish; in this matter people have different boiling points. But efforts and resistances and anguish there must be—or refusals to make efforts and resistances, with anguish either way inevitable.

1.

From the Church Christ wanted to the Church Christ got the plunge looks fearful. But he knew it would be so.

At the Last Supper he warned Peter that he would betray him three times before the next dawn; he told the others, "You will all fall away because of me this night" (Matt. 26:31).

Earlier he had warned the men he was training that scandals would come, and the punishment of one who causes Christ's little ones to sin is fierce—"better for him to have a great millstone tied round his neck and be drowned in the depth of the sea." In Luke 20:46 he is more specific. Luke leads into the warning with the strange phrase, "*In the hearing of all the people* he said to his disciples, 'Beware of the scribes' "; then Christ proceeds to list some of the faults he is warning them against—hypocrisy, vanity, greed for money. Paul will later describe the priests of the new Church in much the same terms. Yet Christ had already entrusted his whole mission and messge to these men—their commands and prohibitions would be validated in heaven; and Paul had called the Church "the household of God . . . the pillar and the bulwark of the truth" (I Tim. 3:15).

In full knowledge of what men are, in full knowledge of what these particular men were, in full knowledge of what these particular men had just done, Christ made them the first officials of his Church: "Going teach all nations, baptizing them in the name of the Father and of the Son and of the Holy Spirit, teaching them to observe all that I have commanded you, and lo, I am with you always to the end of the age."

Why, knowing men, did he entrust so much to them? There seems to be only one answer. He wanted his gifts of truth and life and union with himself brought to the whole world till the end of time. As he saw it, that needed an organization functioning among men if it was to be done effectively. Therefore, he had no choice. He must use men. The Holy Spirit would guide them, but they were still men—minds of their own, wills of their own. One of the first dozen he chose sold him to death.

Consider a man baptized as an adult: he has acquired the new powers described in a previous chapter—faith, hope, charity, prudence, justice, temperance, fortitude. And they are real powers. Yet he has to set them operating in the nature he already has. Let us suppose him with two special weaknesses—he lusts for women, he is by nature pessimistic. He has just acquired the virtue of hope, and as he leaves the baptismal font life may never have looked blacker; he has just acquired the virtue of temperance, and he may be longing for a woman as he has never longed.

The natural tendency is a fact, the new powers are facts. How to make them all work together? The conflict may be lifelong, with many upswings, many falls. Yet the new powers are real powers, even if he cannot make his nature respond. It is like a great pianist with an untuned piano: it is no defect of his musicianship that he cannot make music with that piano. He may produce nothing but distressing noises. And it is no use to work harder on his musical gift, he must mend the piano. Metaphors of this sort are seldom perfect, but this one strikes me as close to precise. At least it helps us see the problem clearer.

Our nature is the piano. Some of what may look like the grossest sins may lie deep woven in the nature we were born with, genes and such, made worse by the way we ourselves have misused it. It is not enough, though it is essential, to try to increase our grace, by sacraments for instance—the confessional and the altar rail. We have to work on our nature, on the union of body and spirit that each of us is. There is no spiritual shortcut to getting rid of bad habits. Only hard toil against them, trying not to give way to them, repenting our failures, dusting off the knees of our trousers after every fall, starting again—with confession to a priest, if we know that this is Christ's will for us.

In all this we have one strong reason why Christ tells us not to judge. We must not condemn others—because we cannot see their genes! We must not abandon ourselves as hopeless—we cannot see our own genes either! Self-condemnation could turn pessimism, a defect of temperament, into despair.

Part of our difficulty in tuning the piano which is our nature, is that often we do not realize how badly out of tune it is. Here the confessional helps. Quite apart from the grace of the sacrament, the mere putting of our sins into words to tell them to another man helps us to get the smell of them as nothing else in my experience does. Yet even with confession, even more without it, we fool ourselves all too easily about the evil we do, the good we don't. A priest once told me that in long years in the confessional, he had never heard anyone confess unkindness!

The trouble is that we are used to our own sins; they do not shock us as other people's sins do. I do not know how often I have quoted the seventeenth-century Samuel Butler's lines—about people who—

> Compound for sins they are inclined to
> By damning those they have no mind to.

Not a week passes but I catch someone, myself occasionally, doing just that. When it is myself I snap out of it, thanks to Butler. But he is not known widely enough. Too many inveigh against the evils in society because it takes their mind off the evils in themselves—they feel better, as if they had done something: just indignation gives the illusion of justice. So with the reprobation of other's sins, which happen not to be our own. One can work oneself up to a high state of indignation and return to the enjoyment of one's own sins with a sense of the good fight well fought.

A person of the type just described we may think of as an immature Christian or a less mature human being; he tells himself that God does not really mind what he's doing, perhaps that God is not looking. For the most part he cuts off communication with God, doesn't talk to him till the temptation is over, then resumes communication with or without a muttered apology. The more mature sinner knows his guilt, sees its folly, keeps up such relation with Christ as he can manage, hopes for mercy, doesn't pretend to give up his sin until he actually does. He is not fooling himself into thinking he is fooling God. He may even quote to himself, "Do not to be deceived, God is not mocked."

"Seeing its folly—" that is at least a beginning. But by itself it may only make his sense of guilt more acute, without making the temptation more resistible. Can grace help? Which means can Christ? Can the Holy Spirit?

2.

Can Christ help? He has warned us of the evils that flow from any passion out of control: has he any contribution to our controlling it? To that question the answer is instant: Yes. But what is his contribution? There is no instant answer to that. But what's the hurry? The problem will be with each of us for a long time. It will call for an understanding and a remaking of ourselves in relation to God, to Christ, and to our fellow humans. At every point Christ will help us. And the light we get will fall upon the whole matter, not only upon sex, which makes a useful blackboard model for all of them: because it is so all-but-universal, and its symptoms are so very evident.

I need hardly tell anyone that conversion to Christ does not automatically make us virtuous. Yet we might have expected a new life to be more instantly, even spectacularly, effective than it usually is.

Listen to Paul: "With Christ I have been crucified; it is no longer I who live but Christ who lives in me" (Gal. 2:20). That was Paul's way of saying the unsayable, uttering the glory of rebirth in Christ. In that instant he was thinking only of the central reality, not of the weakness of the self into which the glory had been set flaming. It was sheer ecstasy, but the weakness remained and had to be coped with. "I chastise my body and bring it into subjection, lest after preaching to others I should myself be cast away" (1 Cor. 9:27).

That, we feel, sounds more like you and me. But let us spell out the cry of ecstasy. It has a bearing on us too. In what sense had Paul, and you and I, been crucified with Christ?

We are back to that fearful moment in the Garden when the weight of our sins was laid on him and brought him close to death; in a way beyond our understanding he had been given the awareness—vision, feel, smell—of the unloveliness of the mankind for love of which he was dying. This was the cup he had asked his Father might pass from him. And it did not pass. "There came an angel from heaven strengthening him"—to endure it! After that it was that the sweat poured out of him as blood pours.

It seems certain that the agony did not leave him till life did. With not only the torturers and the mockers actually there to remind him of mankind's unloveliness, there was this vaster burden weighing him down. "He himself bore our sins in his body on the tree," says Peter, "that we might die to sin and live to righteousness" (1 Pet. 2:24). That was the sense in which Paul and all of us were on the Cross with him.

And it is into the Christ who bore our sins, rose again, and ascended to his Father, that Paul and we are reborn. He lives in us, we live in him. All is clear—enough!—save

Paul's "I live, *now not I.*" It goes with his "put off the old self." Our sins are clearly remains of the "old self," the original I, which can give us the impression that it is completely in charge! Yet once we are reborn in Christ, we really are a new man, a new creature, unless we cut ourselves off from his Body by definitely rejecting him. We are still in the stream of his life—it flows up to us and around us: we may have barred ourselves against its inflow by serious sin: but the entry may always be unbarred by genuine repentance.

We can summarize this: Just as Christ's divinity spared him nothing, so our membership of his Body spares us nothing: we still have to make our own efforts. He will aid us, but the efforts must be our own.

So how does he aid us?

First, by helping us to see the reality in which we are, and in relation to which decisions have to be made, temptations fought, our wills brought under control. This is what St. Paul meant in saying, "We have the mind of Christ"—the *nous* in Greek, the knowing faculty: enlightened by him, we are living mentally in the same world as he, the real world—not simply the patch of grass immediately under our noses; not even the larger area into which our own particular powers and interests would naturally lead us; but the totality—all things whatever related to God and so to one another—life here and life hereafter. It is of this world that the moral laws Christ gives us are the laws: living mentally in this world we see why they are its laws.

We are in fact back to the first condition of living intelligently, set out in chapter four, knowing what life is about—why we are here, where we are supposed to be going, how we are to get there. We are now on the last of these, namely, how to get there—the rules for life on the road. We know from Christ what the rules are, where their observance leads us, where their ignoring. We have seen what human beings are and what their sacredness— as having an immortal spirit, made in God's image, redeemed by Christ. We have grasped why sex is sacred as the way of bringing such beings into life, a way in which God depends upon our cooperation so that he will not produce new generations without it, and gives us a sacrament to help us live up to our commitment to himself, to each other, and to the race.

Common sense might at least have told us that sex is for generation as lungs for breathing—if humans were not meant to breathe or to procreate they would not have had lungs or sexual organs, a reflection which should at least give us pause about cutting sex activity totally off from procreation. Common sense is a marvelous gift, a pity it's so rare. In any event, Christ has not left us solely to it. He has left us in no doubt of the sacredness of sex, about the defilement which follows its misuse.

Yet—knowing all that, seeing their own foolishness with dazzling clarity—believers can misuse sex so very variously. Lust can dazzle even more. When it is in charge, nothing else can be seen save dimly. Knowledge alone will not carry men through as against either lust or any other passion.

Only a vital relation with Christ can, and in that lies the second way in which he helps—through the Holy Spirit, who is his gift to us. Grace has no direct access to our bodily organs, but it has direct access to our very selves, our intellects, and our wills. If we have made the long slow effort of habituation we can come to see Christ closer and clearer, to the point where setting our wills against his can look to us as monstrous as it is. And that is a vast help.

That degree of realization is perhaps rarer than quite genuine faith. The test of faith is the willingness to die for it. The test of realization is the strength of the desire to live up to it. I think many a martyr has triumphantly passed the death test, who had felt the living-up test almost beyond him!

Knowledge is not enough, nor even realization. Over both, almost in a different category, is a love of Christ in which the love into which we have been reborn has at last drawn fully into union with itself the love which is ours as human beings. The will, God aiding, has brought its two loves into harmony. In its perfection this may be rare. But even the "felt" love of Christ which is a driving element in it, would make him a sure point of return after separation by sin, and might bring us to a repentance having in it something of the intensity that legend attributes to Peter's—the tears he shed cutting great furrows in his face.

3.

In any study of Christ's guide to moral health, many people will gain more from a careful reading of the parables than from his teaching on the major sins we have been looking at.

The parables have two major themes—the kingdom

and the individual sinner. The two can interweave, of
course. But it is of the second sort that I am thinking. Each
treats of nameable wrongdoing—the unpleasing person
who showed no mercy when great mercy had been shown
himself (Matt. 18:34); the servant who beat the other
servants and went on drinking parties (Luke 30); the
servant who wasted his employer's goods (Luke 16); the
son who left home and lived riotously (Luke 15); the
clergy who passed by on the other side (Luke 10); the
shepherds (John 10) who ran away when the wolf came
(there were eleven shepherds in training who might have
blushed to tell that parable in later years).

There is nothing very spectacular here, nothing that
would make the front page of a newspaper—no slayings,
no slanderings or false witnessing, no adulteries or forni-
cations, even though drinking parties and riotous living
might have palled without any such. Our Lord is not
treating of the great sinner but of the average sinner—
powers lying unused, immoderate pleasure grabbed at,
the self its own rule.

The ultimate purpose of biology is health. Health
means not simply the absence of any of the major diseases,
or even of the nameable minor ills. It means all parts of the
organism being as they should and functioning as they
should. We might have a clean bill of health, yet feel
all-overish. Someone tells us of a new vitamin just discov-
ered further down the alphabet; perhaps that will do the
trick.

In the biology I am sketching of our life in Christ, the
big sins, the labelable sins, and even the little (but still
nameable) ones have been touched on. We might have

them all under control, yet not feel well. For spiritual health, like bodily, is not the absence of disease but fullness of life. If only there were a spiritual vitamin we could take, in the Greek alphabet perhaps, somewhere between Alpha and Omega. Having nothing we can name in the confessional, we may be reduced to telling a sin of our past life. The experience is not unknown of coming out of confession with a word of commendation from the confessor, yet feeling a cheapness about oneself, a shoddiness.

I do not pretend to know the remedy. I wish I did. But the condition is so common that even a small light on it might be welcome.

No doubt all the thou-shalt-nots have struck roots deep in our psyches. We do not find any obvious breaches of the Commandments, so we assume all is well. But the old rule *bonum est diffusivum sui* is still true—the good tends to spread; that is good's nature. Healthy powers want action. With love of God and neighbor alive, our self-examination would contain not only what ill have I done, but what good, not strictly required of me, could I have done and did not do?

We should be as rigorous on the second part of the examination as on the first (though that too might do with some tightening up). What opportunities for effort or sacrifice have come my way today? Did I do nothing? Did I do too little? We might remember the unhappy people we might have encouraged, but didn't, to tell of their unhappiness at length; the destitute people, their problems known to us, and ourselves hesitating whether to give them ten dollars or would five be enough; the ex-

believers whom, with a little Christian sympathy, we
might have brought a little closer to Christ. . . .

"Weariness in well doing" was a temptation we used to
be warned against. Our present problem is not exactly
"weariness"—most of us have not done enough good to
induce fatigue—but the absence of any urge to do more,
indeed of the faintest awareness that we should. But for
our invulnerable innocence, our guilt might be considerable.

Situations of that sort do from time to time confront us.
How well we meet them will depend on what the general
run of our life has made of us. The way we meet them
affects our own personal relation with Christ, and to that
extent we may regard it as our own (and his?) affair. But if,
because of us, another man or woman sees the face of
Christ harder, with no pity in it, because that was the face
we showed him, then we have served our Saviour ill.
Certainly there have been whole periods when the suffering face of Christ seemed to be on the heretic, with Christians wielding the scourges. It is tough on us, but inescap-
able, that people will judge Christ by Christians. We did
not ask for so heavy a responsibility but his followers carry
it with them wherever they are known. The judging never
stops, of individuals, of the Church.

Of the Church especially. And specially by its members. Let us take one more look at that. We complain of
the sermons? But what single man or woman out of the
hundreds we meet, have we ourselves ever taught about
one single element in the message of Christ? Such and
such a bishop, I have actually heard the phrase, makes
one ashamed of being a Catholic. From what eminence of

virtue do we judge him as beneath us? We are the Church as much as the hierarchy is.

The world may judge Christ ill because of pope or hierarchy. But my personal world may judge Christ ill because of me. The Church's teaching or example may need reforming. But the one member of the Church whose reform I can do something about is me ("I," you murmur grammatically: have it your own way: as long as each of us does something about it).

4.

We have now drawn our picture of man. We have already seen what a difference it would make to all the problems now rending our world if we all took it as matter of fact that every man (ourself included) has an immortal element in him and is made in God's image. If we add that Christ died for every man, the picture is complete. If we realized this, if it were not simply in the mind's files so that we could look it up if the question arose, but so built into our actual awareness that we never saw a man or woman without seeing the immortality, the image of God, the blood Christ shed—then we simply could not go on treating people as we tend to.

We tend to see them as lovable if we happen to find them so; interesting if we happen to find them so; usable for our own pleasure or profit if we happen to find them so. Apart from these possibilities we hardly see people at all, unless some disaster forces individuals or groups on our attention, in which event we discover and release incredible store of generosity and sacrifice in ourselves.

Wordsworth could say:

> *To me the meanest flower that blows can give*
> *Thoughts that do often lie too deep for tears.*

That of course was Wordsworth: he responded to flowers. How many of us could say the same about "the merest human being that breathes"? Only St. Francis, perhaps, or saints of his quality. Yet neither the meanest of flowers nor the most gorgeous compares with the splendor, however encrusted or distorted, that goes into the being of any man or woman whatever—if only we would choose to let ourselves *see* the truths Christ has put at our disposal about humanity.

Nothing tests our love like our fellow Christians. People who can discuss religion amicably with Mohammedans, Buddhists, Parsees, Confucians, find it difficult to keep their tempers with people they know to be believers in the same Christ—Catholics with Protestants, Protestants with Catholics. It gets worse with coreligionists. I do not know how Protestants are with Protestants, but some of the fiercest infighting ever seen is between Catholics and Catholics.

Even saints.

Knowing the situation in the thirteenth century, we feel a certain satisfaction in hearing St. Catherine of Siena call some of the cardinals "not men but devils, in love with the foulness of their own bodies." I quote from memory, but I have not made it worse than she said it. Did it give her satisfaction too? I do not mean pious satisfaction, but good, juicy, earthy satisfaction of the "that's telling them" sort? Did she, when she had cooled down, feel that in her anger she had sinned against charity? Did she tell it in confession? She may, for all I know, have done precisely that. If she didn't, should she have? Not for me to say. I merely note that it is hard to imagine St. Francis talking like that. But then she got the popes back from Avignon, one can't see him doing anything of the sort.

Having started this line, I find myself wondering about St. Paul (whom I revere to the limit). After his row with Barnabas—"paroxysm" is the Greek word (Acts 15:39)—after he had withstood Peter to the face (for weakening in the matter of eating with the Gentile Christians) (Gal. 2:11)—did he, either time, feel contrition at having enjoyed his anger too much? Who knows? I merely remind myself that Our Lord's advice, "Be angry and sin not," is very tough in the observance.

And too often, when their coreligionists do not see eye to eye with them, Christians do not feel called on to make the effort.

Especially saints?

The Book of Common Prayer summarizes all the elements that fight against Christ's life in us by the counter-trinity, the World, the Flesh, and the Devil.

The Flesh—human nature unredeemed, the nature we brought with us to our rebirth—has been treated at what you may regard as inordinate length. Remain the other two.

As the devil or Satan or Beelzebub or prince of this world, you will meet him close on sixty times in the Gospels. I have never heard any argument with even a thread of force in it against the possibility that spiritual beings might exist with no material element. In chapter three we looked at Our Lord's certainty both of the existence of the devil and of his dangerousness.

As the Crucifixion came closer he spoke of it increasingly as the moment of decision between himself and Satan. A Christian would want strong reason to brush Christ aside on this matter.

Why then do I not treat him in detail? Because, with all warnings from Christ and Peter and John, we never seem to catch him at it! There is no open attack. Their own will to self will be drawing men the way he wants them to go. It does seem possible that easing them along that way is all he feels necessary with most. Men of power—of political power like rulers, social power like thinkers, moral power like saints—would concern him more. But who knows?

So we are left with the third in the shadow trinity—the World.

CHAPTER ELEVEN

The World

1.

Worldliness does indeed dim the mind which should be receiving light from Scripture. It distorts the mind's seeing, just as it corrodes the will's decision-making. We all see its unreality; we should hate to admit ourselves worldly, but only the greatest saints have been free from it and it is the last weakness many of them had to conquer. St. Paul calls it "the fashion of this world"—to which we must not be "conformed." Scripture is filled with superb statements of its foolishness, its sinfulness. "All flesh is grass, all its beauty is like the flower of the field. The grass withers, the flower fades"—one sees why Peter quoted these words of Isaiah in his own first Epistle. The poets match Scripture's realism and sometimes its superbness—

> The glories of our blood and state
> Are shadows not substantial things
> There is no armour against fate
> Death lays his icy hand on kings.

We accept Scripture and the poets, taking pleasure in the realism, rejoicing in the verbal skill.

137

Yet after every one of them, there is a primordial something in us which says its own discordant "But . . . ."
Flesh is indeed as grass—but in flesh aflame there is
nothing herbal. Earth's glories are indeed shadows—but
"what lovely things these shadows be." Human life, we
hardly need to be reminded, is not even a split second on
the cosmic clock: but we are not living by the cosmic
clock: and in the clock of our own inbuilt dailiness, it can
feel a very long time indeed. Mohammed says truly that
this life of ours is less than the beat of a gnat's wing; and so
it is in comparison with eternity: but eternity is not on
hand for comparison; we, living from moment to moment,
find that the gnat and its wingbeat do not translate easily
into our experience.

Neither, certainly, did Mohammed. The poets and the
Scripture writers have to come down from their mount of
transfiguration and be their daily selves, the world pressing in on them as on the rest of us. When Paul said, "Be
not conformed to the fashion of this world that passes," he
was talking not only to the Corinthians: he was talking to
Paul. He knew about the sting in his flesh, which he had
vainly begged God to take from him. But did he know how
stung he was by the sneers about him which he quotes (2
Cor. 10:10), "His appearance, they say, is mean and his
speech contemptible"? Or am I wrong in feeling his hurt,
over the centuries?

The world, we observe, never defends itself against its
critics: it just goes right on, pressing in on us, on its critics
themselves, as it pressed in on and pressured Christ. He
resisted it, preserved his integrity wholly. Most of us
resist fitfully, with nothing like the mobilizing of mind

and will and emotion that a pressure so unrelaxing calls for.

The mind, particularly, should be fully engaged, and on two fronts. First, it must "sift" the world, sorting out the good from the bad in what the world offers it, the healthful from the poisonous, things essential to be used from things essential to be avoided, the building things, the destroying things: second, the mind must study itself to see how the evil of the world has already seeped into it unnoticed.

This is the harder of the two, because the seepage began the moment we ourselves began—in the genes, in the womb, in the cradle, the seepage and we began together. Only a very able mind is likely to question what has always been in it, what one's own country or class takes for granted: the customary has all the laws's nine points of possession—unless it causes us pain.

In relation to Christ, we are not so likely to be overborne by the world's doubts—at least they come at us structured and stated. But we can be affected—unawares again—by the world's emphases, what matters a lot and what matters a little, what we must affirm against the world at all costs and what we can come to regard as our own private concern, to be kept within ourselves, and affirmed only by nondenial.

With nondenial we are facing the toughest point of the world's threat—our overrespect for its opinion. So assured is the world at any given moment of its own rightness that to speak our Christian mind openly in its presence takes a courage which not all of us have—even when we remember that Christ said, "Whoever denies me be-

fore men, him also will I deny before my Father" (Matt.
10:33). People who would face torture in the arena rather
than deny him, cannot bring themselves to affirm him at
the dinner table against the amused smile, the raised
eyebrow, of the unbeliever. Our silence spares us the
smile and the eyebrow, and eats away at the vitality of our
belief.

In my own lifetime we have passed from silence of that
evading sort, through open affirmation, back to silence
and evasion. The first state I have described in *The
Church and I*—the stage at which Carlyle could say that
Cardinal Newman had the brain of a moderate-sized rab-
bit: Newman could take that sort of sneer unruffled and
come right back: William George Ward, who had helped
Newman into the Church, could meet John Stuart Mill
with an eyebrow raised as high as his. But Catholics
generally had a feeling that while they had the Faith the
world had the arguments and it was better just to stay
with Mass and sacraments and avoid argument. In Eng-
land, Belloc and Chesterton, in France, Péguy and Bloy,
stirred Catholics out of their silence, and we emerged into
fifty years of unembarrassed affirmation.

But now the first stage is returning, against a new form
of pressure not only from the unbelieving world but from
within the Church—the extreme right raging against all
change as heresy, the extreme left sneering at all they
dismiss as traditional. For the moment I am not discussing
who is right and who is wrong—only urging that when
such matters arise we ask ourselves what our own silence
means. It may be a quite correct admission of our incom-
petence. It may be evasion, or in plain words, cowardice.

Yet not necessarily, not always anyhow, quite that. We
are social beings by nature with powers in us which can be
used, needs in us which can be met, only in relation to
others; and society is a structure in which the powers can
be fruitfully used and the needs to a high level satisfied.
There is an instinct to conform out of a genuine awareness
of what life outside a social order would be, and there can
be a real discomfort in being out of step. Yet even at the
level of ordinary practicality, the instinct to conform must
stand our examining. Samuel Butler, with no personal
God to color his judgment, reminds us that "all progress
arises from the inability of the organism to be content with
its environment."

In other words, the conformity must be judged by the
mind. And so must the progress. Judged by what? In
relation to what?

It goes with human unpredictability that our worldliness is not an absolute. In all of us it is a more and a
less—there are maybe a handful of people at one end of
the scale wholly worldly, a handful at the other with a
marvelously balanced relation to this world and the next.
I'm not dead sure that I've met one at either end of the
scale, though there have been men and women at both
ends who have left me pretty convinced.

But for most people worldliness is not the whole story.
In Albert Camus we can read of the people of Paris as
"four million shadows who read the newspapers and copu-
late." That was a mood (in Camus, I mean, not the Pari-
sians). There would be few of those sex-hungry shadows
who had not a depth in them, loves and hates and dreams
and discontents, with stirrings in it beyond newspapers,

beyond the sexing. H. G. Wells knew it, with his "guttersnipe in love with unimaginable goddesses." And Camus knew it, and built his superb fictional world out of it. The wholly commonplace is less common than the cynic supposes. Those shadows of Camus's had their moments: anyone who has not had such moments had better take a careful look at himself. He is drifting close to humanity's very edge.

That warning is for us too. Moments of that sort can disturb our dailiness but cannot revitalize it. Only reality, seen and accepted, can do that, and the never-relaxed pressure of the world can keep us from the concentration which reality demands. Reality has to be labored for by the mind, whereas the world has its immediacy, its ever-thereness, soliciting the body with its pleasures, harmless and harmful, offering ambition its prizes—we have seen them turn to dust and ashes often enough in other men's mouths, but our mouths are urgent for them.

The danger for the Christian is that he can drift (that word again) into a soothing compromise—not actually denying in words any teachings of Christ, but somehow blunting their point and smoothing their edges so that Mammon is not interfered with. The only remedy is the effort we have already discussed, to concentrate all our mind's seeing power on what Christ is actually saying and our will's energy on living by it.

For another type of Christian the smoothing may present a different danger. He may have been taught by men or women—priests, brothers, nuns—whose concession to worldliness is to smooth away differences, not for Mam-

mon's sake, but for belief's sake: they are honestly convinced that this is the best way to keep people in the
Church. The result is that mystery is gone, with nothing
left that a sensible man could find any difficulty in accept-
ing, nothing left for light or nourishment either, unobjec-
tionable indeed, but not worth having, syrup easily swal-
lowed but not long appetizing. Especially it does not meet
the appetite which all vital minds have for depth. So we
see them going into mystical cults, out of step with a world
which does not know where it is going.

2.

That Christians should see Christ clearly is not just a
luxury for themselves. It is of the first practical importance for everybody. That Christians—born into him at
Baptism, sworn to his service in Confirmation—should
see him only sketchily and hear him only barely, is of
course their personal loss. But it is not only that. It means
first that they are ineffective in a Church which so many of
its members have left and so few are joining: only Christ
actually known can hold the Christians who still hang on
to belief in him, and win back those who have either
slipped out not caring, or stamped out in anger. But it
means also that they are ineffective in a world moving
toward chaos because of needs Christ could help it meet.
    The two thousand million who (according to the Vatican
Council) have never heard of Christ would find this
statement meaningless. Those who *have* heard of him
would dismiss it as merely eccentric—mankind has
reached maturity, they feel, and has no needs it cannot

meet from its own resources.

This notion of mankind come of age and God no longer needed was propounded by Nietzsche in the nineteenth century: it did not save him from lunacy. It gained special currency in this century from its statement by the Lutheran Pastor Bonhoeffer, slain by Hitler. If he was right about mankind's coming of age, we can only say that mankind had a rather spectacular coming-of-age party—how many million Russians (eight? ten?) allowed to starve by Stalin, how many million Jews (five? six?) cremated by Hitler, how many thousand Japanese slain in a couple of flashes by ourselves, a million Americans slain in the womb by people paid by their mothers in the first year of legalized abortion. There are those who would make a case for one or other of these slayings: but none of them sound like maturity. Vatican II was nearer reality when it said that mankind had reached a crisis point on its way to maturity.

What lay behind this feeling of maturity attained? Obviously, the great strides made by technology, leading to a hope that science will straighten it all. But in the conflict between good and evil, science takes no side: it is there to be used by anyone who will give himself the trouble to master its procedures. Yet hope in science remains a slogan, and nothing blinds the mind more than slogans: they have their whole existence in the mouth, the brain not stirring a muscle.

Especially relevant to our present inquiry is the notion that science has answered all the questions religion was invented to answer. No one who has ever lived a religion could think it. Nor, short of living it himself, could anyone who had ever studied religion even as a branch of sociology.

Men's continuing anguishes—the consciousness of our own mediocrity, the friends who fail us, the friends we fail, love unreturned, the sense of going nowhere in particular, our helplessness against political and economic forces we can neither control nor understand, a world growing every day more complicatedly chaotic—to none of these can science bring relief or any hint of remedy. It simply cannot touch them at all. Religion can.

On both of the notions we have lingered over—the maturity mankind thinks it has reached, and the feeling that science is taking over religion's job and handling it better—the Old Testament might have been written as a commentary.

We meet ourselves on every page, and there is nothing in any of the meetings to flatter our sense of a maturity lacking in its writers, flowering in us. Humanity has nowhere else been exposed so naked to its own gaze, its profoundest problems so realistically shown it: all its anguishes are still with us. And no more now than then can the problems be solved or the anguishes healed from within men's own resources. Man is the problem, and problems do not solve themselves.

One would have to be singularly slogan-blunted to think that the discoveries of modern science could be anything but peripheral. It not only does not answer the questions, it is not equipped even to ask them.

Consider Abraham's wife, Sarah, and Abraham's descendant, David.

Abraham had no children. That Abraham might not die without issue, Sarah sent her handmaid Hagar to his bed. Hagar bore Ishmael—and "showed contempt" for her barren mistress. Later, Sarah, too, had a son, Isaac. The jealousy between the two women resulted in Hagar and her son being driven out into the desert to perish. The resentment of one woman, the rage of both, emerge living in chapters 15 and 21 of Genesis. Hagar and her son did not perish. Ishmael lived to be the father of children. The Arabs believe that he is their ancestor. So that three thousand years later the war between Hagar and Sarah is being fought out still—with the Arabs pointing out that their ancestor, Ishmael, was the elder.

Why do I tell the story here? It makes our point. No training in modern science could have prevented Hagar from feeling superior and Sarah from feeling envious, nor once those feelings had arisen could either woman have been helped to act sensibly by knowing that the earth was three thousand million years old or that men would one day be on the moon.

You may think the point has been sufficiently made. But I like thinking about David. We remember his heart-wrung, "Absalom, my son Absalom," when the boy who had gone into rebellion against him was slain. That was David at his (rare) best.

Read the story of Uriah (2 Sam. 11). While he was with the army fighting the Ammonites, his wife, Bathsheba, was pregnant by David. David had him brought back that he might visit his wife and so assume that the child was his. But on account of a vow, Uriah would not visit her. So David sent him back to the army with a letter to the commander—"Set Uriah in the forefront of the fighting, then draw back from him, that he may be struck down and die."

Read chapter 12 for what the prophet Nathan said to
David and how God punished him. I tell the story, partly
for the same reason as for telling of Sarah and Hagar—that
to our real problems and anguishes science has precious
little relevance; they are in the heart of man, the will of
man, to which science has no access.

But there was a special reason for telling this particular
story—namely, Nathan's "You are the man" (12:7). We
may feel that we have never done anything to compare
with David's foulness. But in many an Old Testament
story we can meet ourselves, not looking our best. Sarah
and Hagar were not the first women nor are they likely to
be the last to feel like that about each other. And when
other men's wives are in question, men of honor are no
more to be relied on to act honorably than the lowest cads
they would despise in any other relation.

Knowing ourselves, I have said, is essential to understanding the world's plight. For peoples are governed,
their affairs administered by people like themselves—a
very small chance might have had some of us in their high
places. There are economic problems, scientific problems, the solution of which would make administration
easier. But if the heart is evil, the will clutching and
evading, no system can bring happiness. Christ's whole
concentration was on the healing of the heart. And he
gave the rules for it—love God, love your neighbor, with
the development he gave these in the Sermon on the
Mount and in the parables.

One might dismiss all this as unrealistic. But at least
one cannot deny that if they were lived up to, they *would*
heal. Anyone who has made any serious effort to live by

them knows that they work, knows it by the double test of the good that flows from their performance, and the evil that never fails to follow from their flouting.

As to their being unrealistic—how dare our world call anything unrealistic? Mankind has reached maturity, says Nietzsche and Bonhoeffer and just about everybody. "A crisis point on the way to maturity," warns Vatican II. As things are, the chaos can only get worse, because the rulers have no more idea than the people they rule of what life is all about. Christ could tell them. Someone'must make them aware of Christ.

CHAPTER TWELVE

The End of Our Road

At death we leave the road of life on earth forever. "It is appointed to man to die once, and after that the judgment" (Heb. 9:27).

This moment, like all the decisive moments, has its sacrament. We find it already in action in the early Church. "If any man be sick among you, let him call in the officials of the Church, and let them pray over him, anointing him with oil in the name of the Lord; and the prayer of faith will save the sick man, and the Lord will raise him up; and if he has committed sins, he will be forgiven." So wrote James (5:14).

If we are conscious, there will be confession and Eucharist too. It is no jest to say that ours is a wonderful religion to die in.

1.

The one judgment the New Testament speaks of is the judgment at the end of time—a judgment of the whole human race, the kingdom at last seen in its fullness, with all in it who are to be in it! The whole race, those who have accepted and those who have refused, will be seeing the whole race in its relation to God.

The reader who reads Scripture slowly and closely

149

realizes that God is continuously aware of all mankind as none of its members can be, and that it has a meaning for him that it has not for us. He sees it all, every member of it from the beginning. To us it is too scattered through the myriad of years to be seen at all, save as a general notion. To God this general notion is a wholly particular notion. In various modes he has made his love available to all and longed to have each return his love.

This is the human race Christ agonized for in Gethsemane and died for on Calvary: writing chapter 53, Isaiah could not have imagined what the words, "The Lord has laid on him the iniquity of us all," were actually saying. We may think of the Last Judgment as a spectacle unrivaled. For Christ and his Father it will be a culmination with all meaning in it. Will the question strike them: Was it worth it? The evidence will be there.

Are we to understand that each must wait till the resurrection of the body at the end of time to resume the life ended here by death? Back in the fourteenth century, Pope John XXII thought so and preached so, in several sermons in Avignon, where the papacy then was. The pope was startled by the uproar that filled the theological sky—he had always thought that that was Catholic doctrine. He had the learned Cistercian, Jacques Fournier, instruct him. He reminded him perhaps that Christ had said to the repentant thief on the cross—"This day you will be with me in Paradise": we know what happened to their bodies that day.

Paul lived in the certainty of continuance, with no question save, "How soon?" In his second letter to the

Corinthians (5:6) he had put it succinctly: "While we are at home in the body, we are away from the Lord . . . we would rather be away from the body and at home with the Lord." To the Philippians (1:21) he opened his heart more fully: "For me to live is Christ, to die is gain. If it is to be life in the flesh, that means fruitful labor for me. Yet which I should choose I cannot tell . . . my desire is to depart and be with Christ, for that is far better. But to remain in the flesh is more necessary on your account."

So the Church has always taught that there is no gap. Departed from the body, the soul continues its own spiritual activities. What will these be? That depends on the condition in which each dies. He may love God, and therefore neighbor, with his "whole mind, heart and strength." He may love both genuinely, but with too much of self still clung to, not brought into full union. Or he may have refused love, banked all on self, God ignored or resented, men ignored or exploited.

2.

What is to happen to this one at death? If self-love has really taken over the self, it is hard to see what even God can do with him or even for him. He has banked all on self: all God can do is let him have himself.

What can we know of hell? Gehenna—the Valley of Hinnom—is the Old Testament word: it had become a rubbish dump, worms in it, fires burning. "If your eye causes you to sin, pluck it out: it is better for you to enter the Kingdom of God with one eye than with two eyes to be thrown into hell, where 'their worm does not die, and the

fire is not quenched' " (Mark 9:47). Christ is quoting the
last verse of Isaiah.

On those who refuse aid to the needy, the judgment
will be, "Depart from me into the eternal fire prepared for
the devil and his angels" (Matt. 25:41).

In one of the most famous of parables, the rich man
went to Hades, not specifically hell, but the abode of the
dead—and his torment was thirst (Luke 16:20).

And we have the outer darkness, where there shall be
"weeping and wailing and gnashing of teeth" (Matt.
22:13). All these pains are in the Old Testament, all would
be familiar to his hearers, Christ introduces no new one.
Fire, worms, thirst, darkness, weeping, gnashing of
teeth—gnashing of teeth would seem an odd punishment
for spirits, whether bodiless or disembodied. So would all
the rest: Isaiah indeed was talking not of spirits but of dead
bodies. The actual detail of hell is not describable in terms
of any experience we have had. The eternal failure of a
being with an immortal soul, made in God's image, cannot
be pictured for us. That it *is* failure, and total, can be
conveyed. That is what the images are for. In the modern
phrase, we get the message.

The message leaves us in no doubt that eternal loss is
grievous. Back to the idea of Christ as healer—part of
healing is to make quite clear the evil of the disease
unhealed—and the disease in this instance is refusal to
love, self-love swollen monstrous. Christ does not even
hint at demon-torturers. The suffering is from within the
loveless themselves.

I have said that he introduces no new torment. But he
names one new element—"Depart from me." That is the
whole point—separation from Christ and so from his

Father in heaven—the loveless who have made self their god would find wholly unbearable the immediate presence of the God whose superiority they cannot deny and can only detest. They have banked all on self. They get self. And self is not enough. There are too many powers in them which can be used, so many needs which can be met only in a vital relation with others; the autonomy in which they took their pride was mere blindness. No man is an island: they had lived, each of them, as if he personally was.

Here on earth solitary confinement is horror. And solitude is the continuing condition of those who have shut all others from their love.

To me it seems the name for all this is futility. Perhaps the reality is totally different. May I never find out.

How far can we know if we are moving toward life or loss? It is hard to know how well we love God. But at least of our love of neighbor we can get a fair idea, and that is the one Our Lord most emphasizes. We can put ourselves into the situations he describes as leading away from life—and see how we measure up—the situations we find, for instance, in Matthew 5:27-30, 18:21-35, 25:41-46, Luke 16:19-22.

And there remains the question of our own chapter one—when did we last do something for God or man which really cost us enough to hurt?

3.

In the Sermon on the Mount (Matt. 5:48) Christ said, "You must be perfect as your heavenly Father is perfect." For every being there is a perfection proper to it—man's

is not the same as God's. God is all that God should be.
We are to be, and to have, all that manhood requires for
completeness. The book of Revelation nails it down for
us—"Nothing defiled shall enter heaven." In what does
our perfection consist? In our likeness to God in whose
image man is made. God is love. We must image that. We
cannot *be* love, but we *can* be loving. In the love we give
God and neighbor, Christ places our perfection. Created
beings cannot be infinitely loving, but they can try. Has
anyone who tried ever found the limit? Only those who
have tried can answer that.

I imagine none of us would claim to be perfect at this
moment, all that a man should be, no shadow of defilement? The odds may have struck us as great against our
being so at any moment, including the moment of death.
There is nothing perfecting about dying. If the imperfect
are to come at last to the goal, there must be the possibility of defects being remedied, defilements cleansed after
death. That is what purgatory—from the Latin verb "to
clean"—is for. Christ never speaks of it (though he does
once seem to suggest it, Matt. 12:32). But the Church sees
it as demanded by his demand that we be perfect.

Cleansing is an interlude, heaven is what we are meant
for. "I go to prepare a place for you, that where I am you
may be" (John 14:2-3). He is with his Father. That is
where we are to be. Imagine it as you please. The only
certainty is what Christ has told us about the life there.

The soul, made perfect either at death or by cleansing,
is ready for heaven, the unveiled presence of God. My
guess is that until it was ready, the soul would no more
want to be in, or bear to be in, that presence than weak

eyes would want or bear full sunlight.

But what about judgment? The general judgment of the whole race is somewhere in the future. The Church speaks of a particular, i.e., individual judgment for each. She has given no solemn definition of this. Certainly it is not in the manner of any known judicial proceeding. Oddly enough we get light from what happened to Judas—he "went to his own place" (Acts 1:25). It sounds grisly to us who know what his crime had been. Reading it, we might offer a swift prayer that it might not be said of us. But it will. For it means that we shall go where we belong.

Most scholars, I think, feel that Augustine has seen it right: "My love is my weight": weight decides whether things fall downward or upward: what we love takes us where we belong.

4.

"Will I have my cat—or my whatever it is I can't imagine living without—in heaven?"—that through the ages was the child's question. And "If you want it, you will have it"—that through the ages was the grownup's answer. The grownup knew that the child would grow up out of his present blisses: the child did not know it: both were satisfied. I fancy even grownups have their own slightly less infantile, but infantile still, variant of that question and answer. If they get round to 1 Corinthians they may be startled by Paul's answer to one who asked what life in heaven would be like—"Don't be silly."

We can know nothing of heaven save what Christ tells

us. He does not tell us a great deal, but it is enough to provide a better answer than we may be giving either our children or ourselves, enough to show us the aptness of Paul's impoliteness.

He gives one verb only—the angels of the little ones *"see* the face of my heavenly Father continually." He tells us that in the matter of sexual union in heaven we "shall be like the angels." Paul tells us that in this matter of seeing, too, we shall be like them. "Now we see in a mirror dimly, but there face to face" (1 Cor. 13)—in this life we can see God only as he is "mirrored" in creation, building up such an idea of him as we can; but in heaven we shall see him direct, not even an idea intervening between God and our mind.

In a spiritual being, like our mind, seeing means knowing: any new thing known—even more so any development in our knowing power—enlarges the world we live in, gives a new reason for love, gives new solidity to our decisions, brings us to that extent nearer to maturity. When the new thing known is God seen direct, infinite knowledge, infinite love, then we have at last reached maturity—every power we have in contact with, nourished by, Father, Son, and Holy Spirit.

Till that moment we are still immature, with an immaturity varying from one to another, but in even the most richly endowed, immaturity still. And there is no way of anticipating maturity. "We are God's children now. It does not yet appear what we shall be, but we know that when he appears we shall be like him, for we shall see him as he is" (1 John 3:2).

"We shall see him as he is." What depths we may find in

him we cannot know—the old Greeks and the Hindus and the Zoroastrians and the Chinese may find some of what their own praying and thinking had been reaching toward, they and we rejoicing in it together.

Till we reach maturity we not only cannot know of ourselves what the detail will be like, there is no way in which it could be told to us. Our experience does not provide us even with the language. But maturity we shall at last have reached. We shall be complete men, complete women, instead of the rough sketches of what a man or a woman should be, which even the best of us now is. We shall be complete individually, we shall be a complete community, all in direct contact with the infinite community of the Three-in-One.

What will our activity be? We have no hint. We shall not be gracefully stagnant. For we image God's power too, and so image him in action (which is what Genesis 1 probably had in mind). We are to be the living image of our Father, the image of him living.

There may linger in us a fear that the seen presence of God must produce an atmosphere of the most appalling liturgical solemnity. But we shall not spend eternity rigid with awe. We have been promised joy. And joy will not have a meaning unrelated to any experience of joy we have ever had. Neither will love. Think back on two phrases: "God so loved the world that he gave up his only-begotten Son—to save us from perishing" (John 3:16).

"He did not spare his own Son, but gave him up for us all" (Rom. 8:32).

In other words, his Son's human sufferings were not a matter of infinite indifference to the Father. He cared. He had not less care for his Son than all decent fathers have for the children they love. How the Son loved him we have seen. It was this love of each for the other which produced the Holy Spirit. With Father, Son, and Holy Spirit we shall for the first time know what love is, what joy is.

As you observe, I am writing as if we shall certainly be there. May we all be!